*To read the stars is to read the messages of the Universe.*

*Joni Patry*

# Astrology
# The Divine Order of the Universe

Houses, Numbers, Signs and Planets

Joni Patry

Editing & Publishing services: http://enjoynew.com/en/

Published in Dallas, Texas by Galactic Center
http://www.Galacticcenter.org/
4333 Willow Grove Rd
Dallas, TX 75220
Printed in the United States of America
Second Edition

ISBN-13: 978-0692523520
ISBN-10: 0692523529

*I dedicate this book to my two older sisters,*

*Marsha and Carol*

*who together initiated me into the teachings of*

*Paramahasa Yogananda.*

*The great guru that blended the spirituality of the east with the west*

*and gave me my start in Vedic astrology.*

# Contents

# Charts

# Introduction

This is not your ordinary astrology book on the houses. Many books appeal to the novice to just memorize the meaning of planets, signs and houses. But this book is very different in the effect that it is meant to *activate the mind to truly understand the meanings that make astrology work*. With an understanding of these meanings the entire Universe opens through a mystical experience. The true purpose of astrology is to understand the self, which is the core of the Universe. This in essence is the law of nature and numbers. Numbers are simply the measure of vibration that directs life. They determine the process of the journey of life. Astrology is the study of numbers, signs, houses and planets. This will teach the connection of everything and everyone in life.

To understand the meaning of the houses is to understand astrology and the Universal plan and Divine Order. The houses are the framework and experience of life. Every human experience falls into a category of a house. And there is a pattern or order as we pass through these experiences from birth to death. When we understand the order of the life cycles the Universe begins to make sense.

Astrology is the most ancient and powerful of all the sciences because it encompasses all of science. Astrology is math, numbers, geometry, physics, astronomy, mythology, psychology, and spirituality.

My love of Eastern philosophy brought me to Vedic astrology. I was drawn at an early age to the teachings of Paramahansa Yogananda. As a student of astrology in my teenage years I discovered Paramahansa Yogananda's guru Swami Sri Yukteswar was an astrologer. I later discovered that he practiced Vedic astrology, which was different than Western astrology. So I set out on the journey to learn the astrology the great seers practiced. From then my readings took on a much deeper meaning and I truly began to understand the meaning of numbers and cycles.

The oldest references to astrology in India came from the ancient spiritual texts of India, the Vedas. These spiritual teachings date back to 1,500-2,000 BCE. There are references to certain nakshatras, which are a major component of Vedic astrology. The Vedas are written in hymns and refer other 'Maha Purusha', meaning body of man, and astrology is referred as the eyes of man. This means astrology has the power to give sight.

The deepest wisdom comes from experience. This book is the enfoldment of my studies of astrology and represents self-discoveries personal and collective through living the many astrological meanings through a lifetime.

I have lived the astrological meanings throughout my 30 years of experience. I know what Saturn's transit over the Ascendant feels like when my mother died. I know what Jupiter's transit in the 5th house means as I discovered I was pregnant. I know the experience of falling in love and marriage as Venus and Jupiter aspected the 5th and 7th houses. I observed Ketu as it transited over the Sun and my father died. My mother had Saturn transiting over her Moon in the 8th house as my father, her husband of over 50 years died. I lived through great financial losses when Saturn transited over my Moon ruler of my 2nd house. I have lived the cycles of the planets through my chart and understand from knowing and feeling what it brings, and this can only come through experience.

My knowledge keeps growing and advancing opening the mind more to the infinite knowledge of the Universe, which is the study of astrology.

In this book I refer to the *Sidereal zodiac* used in Vedic astrology. Western astrology uses the Tropical zodiac. The Sidereal zodiac is based on the stars which are slowly moving backwards through the zodiacal signs. This movement is called Precession of the Equinoxes. The tropical zodiac is based on a fixed zodiac that doesn't move and is relative to the sun's movement that creates the seasons. But no matter what system of astrology used the houses will still have the same meanings. So this understanding can be used in Sidereal or Tropical astrology.

But the rulers of the houses and the power a planet in the chart can only be referred to in the sidereal Vedic chart for the planet's signs will be different. The planets and ascendant will be different based on the fact that everything reverts back about 23-24 degrees in backward motion in the zodiac from the tropical placements.

The meaning of the houses from Vedic philosophy is defined through the houses relationship to the signs. There are 12 signs that are relative to the 12 houses. From the start of Aries through Pisces the signs are numbered and their number is relative to the same number of the house.

| | | |
|---|---|---|
| 1. | Aries | =1st House |
| 2. | Taurus | = 2nd House |
| 3. | Gemini | = 3rd House |
| 4. | Cancer | = 4th House |
| 5. | Leo | = 5th House |
| 6. | Virgo | = 6th House |
| 7. | Libra | = 7th House |
| 8. | Scorpio | = 8th House |
| 9. | Sagittarius | = 9th House |
| 10. | Capricorn | = 10th House |
| 11. | Aquarius | = 11th House |
| 12. | Pisces | = 12th House |

The elements and their qualities give specific meanings to the signs and houses, as they are a very important component to the world and life.

The **elements** to the sign/houses are *fire, earth, air, and water*.

The **qualities** of the signs/houses are *cardinal, fixed, and mutable*.

The manner in which the houses are organized is not the sequential order of 1-12, but is divided into segments that give more meaning to understand the houses on a deeper level. The elements are related to the four aims of life – the purpose of man's life.

The four **Aims of life** are *Dharma/Fire, Artha/Earth, Kama/Air, and Moksha/water*. From this analysis the purpose of life emerges.

The application of what each house means based on its relation to all the other houses is delineated in *Bhavat Bhavam*. Which is the power of each house repeated, 1st from the 1st, 2nd from the 2nd, 3rd from the 3rd, 4th from the 4th, 5th from the 5th, 6th from the 6th, 7th from the 7th, 8th from the 8th, 9th from the 9th, 10th from the 10th, 11th from the 11th and 12th from the 12th.

The planets as they rule a house are then placed in another house which connects one house to another and adds a dimension of meaning to a chart.

Another variable to be considered is the power of certain signs. The planets gain or lose power in certain signs. This can make a big difference in the effects of the planets.

The signs planets rule are vitally important in understanding which houses are connected. The ruler of a house is the planet that rules the sign on the house in question. The planets are the energy, the signs give meaning and power, and the house is the area of life that the experiences take place.

Meanings of the houses are relative to numbers and the meanings interrelate to one another, this is what gives each house its meanings. This will be observed through life's experiences and our interconnection to everything and everyone. This is astrology in action the study of humanity. The meaning and understanding this will bring personally is transformational.

There are two charts in each chapter on famous personalities to further explain meanings for the houses being studied.

The last chapter looks at the planets as they transit through the houses to make future predictions.

The nine planets are used, with the old rulerships, Mars rules Scorpio, Saturn rules Aquarius, and Jupiter rules Pisces. The outer planets are transpersonal and reflect larger generations. They have personal effects but influence many born in the same era, both personally and collectively.

The most mystical number of all is 108. This is because 9 planets in all 12 houses equal 108 interpretations. Another reason 108 is so important is that there are 9 divisions of a sign called navamshas and there are 12 signs that are divided 9 times, meaning there are 108 navamshas to the chart. This is a deeper aspect of the numerological meanings relative to Vedic astrology.

As I referred to the outer planets indicating the mass level of consciousness I have noticed that now people are ready and are understanding astrological concepts like never before which means there has been a breakthrough in the consciousness here and now on planet earth.

*Namaste, in peace and love,*

*Joni Patry*

# The Bhavas (Houses)

*Myths are public dreams, dreams are private myths.*

*Joseph Campbell*

The Sanskrit word bhava means *"a field of action"*. There are twelve houses in a chart. Each house defines a different area of life. A thorough understanding of what each house means will give your analysis great depth and accuracy.

The qualities of the houses are explained in terms of angles (kendras), trines (trikonas), upachayas, dusthanas, and marakas. Also the four aims of life: dharma, artha, kama, and moksha give the houses a deeper meaning.

Each house is 30 degrees, so is a sign. The houses in Vedic astrology contain the whole sign. The degree of the ascendant (lagna), the sign rising on the eastern horizon at birth, will be contained within the 1st house.

Since each sign has a ruling planet, the planet that rules the sign contained in the house will be the ruler (lord) of that house. The planets possess certain qualities relative to the houses that they rule. The ruler of a house and the house it resides in determines how the indications for that house will manifest in life. The ruler of a good house, a trikona, (1, 5, and 9) will always bring blessings to the house it occupies. The ruler of a dusthana house (6, 8, and 12) will bring trouble to the house it occupies. Malefic planets ruling good houses can operate as functional benefics, and benefics ruling difficult houses can become functional malefics.

The house position of the ruling planet will link the meanings of these houses. The ruling planet will always carry the meaning of the house/houses it rules. An example would be the ruler of the 5th house in the 9th, giving the mind (5th house) spiritual tendencies (9th house).

Complicating matters is the fact that all planets, excluding the Sun and Moon rule two houses and therefore carry the meaning of both house rulerships. If the ruler of the 5$^{th}$ house also rules the 12$^{th}$ house, as with Gemini and Sagittarius ascendants, and is still placed in the 9$^{th}$, there would be a mixed result. The 9$^{th}$ house is infused with qualities of both the 5$^{th}$ and 12$^{th}$ houses. Since the 9$^{th}$ house can refer to the father this implies loss (12$^{th}$ house) and intelligence (5$^{th}$ house) as some of the features of this person's father. Traditionally if a planet rules a trikona house (1, 5, and 9) and the other house is a more difficult house like a dusthana (6, 8, and 12) the trikona will predominate, but it will not completely override the dusthana meaning. As in the previous example the father (9$^{th}$ house) will be of high intelligence (5$^{th}$ house) but may have to travel (9$^{th}$ house) extensively, and this would give the feeling of loss (12$^{th}$ house) to the children (5$^{th}$ house) because of his absence. The sense of loss is not necessarily from something bad. The planet and the sign will add more details.

For Gemini ascendant the planet would be Venus in Aquarius, which could indicate involvement in the arts with teaching. As for Sagittarius the planet ruling the 5$^{th}$ and 12$^{th}$ would be Mars, which would give a more mechanical aggressive edge, possibly indicating that the father had dealings with engineering or the military. These are just a taste of all the variables that must be assessed when working with houses and house rulerships.

## Categories for the Houses

### Trikona

The trikona houses are 1, 5 and 9. These are the most auspicious houses of all. They give fortune and luck. They are five houses away from each other and form a triangle with each other. The four elements fire, earth, air, and water all form a trine to one another.

The fire element is our dharma. Dharma is our sense of purpose. When we understand our purpose we are connected to our spirit and guided by inspiration. It is the spirit that fuels our life. The trikona houses are the houses related to the fire element, our spirit and inspiration. The 1$^{st}$ house is related to the 1$^{st}$ fire sign Aries, the 5$^{th}$ to Leo, and the 9th to Sagittarius.

## Kendra

The kendra houses are the angles of the chart. These houses are 1, 4, 7 and 10 and are considered the most powerful houses of all. They create the most change and action in a chart. They relate to the qualities of the cardinal signs: 1 - Aries, 4 - Cancer, 7 - Libra, and 10 - Capricorn. These are the houses that bring results. This is why planets that rule a kendra and a trikona house coming together can create the fulfillment of purpose (dharma). This is called Raja Yoga.

**Planets in the kendra houses are very strong and active. But when malefic planets rule the angles they are said to lose their power to cause harm, and when benefic planets rule the angles they lose their power to give blessings.**

## Upachaya

Upachaya means "improvement". The upachaya houses are 3, 6, 10 and 11. They create a certain amount of tension that drives one to improve life's situations. These houses have a competitive edge to them. Life evolves and gets better over time with these houses.

## Dusthana

The dusthana houses are 6, 8 and 12. These houses primarily deal with suffering, and mainly ill health. They are the most difficult of all, ruling disease, death, loss and sorrow. The rulers of these houses will inflict this type of suffering.

Dusthanas are difficult points because they are places of transition. Both the 6th and the 8th are on either side of the 7th house, which is the point of sunset (endings), while the 12th is the shift after the new dawn (beginnings), the ascendant. These houses are sometimes referred to as the *Trik* houses (the Three).

## Maraka

The maraka houses are 2 and 7. Maraka means "killer". These houses and the planets that rule them are considered the killer houses or planets. They are prominent through the dashas or transits when death or injury occurs, but there must be additional determining influences to indicate such an event.

# The Four Aims of Life
## Dharma, Artha, Kama, and Moksha

In Vedic astrology there are four main aims or goals that we aspire to in life. Dharma is our sense of purpose. Artha is the acquisition of wealth. Kama means "desire" and deals with emotional fulfillment. Moksha means "liberation" and refers to spiritual transformation.

## Dharma

The dharma houses are 1, 5 and 9. They relate to the three fire signs (*fire triplicity*). The 1st house relates to the first fire sign Aries the fifth Leo and the ninth Sagittarius

These houses define our sense of purpose and the spirit that moves us. The 1st house is the self, our sense of who we are our spirit. The 5th house is the inspiration of our sense of purpose through creative expression. The 9th house is our spiritual beliefs and truths, the realization of our spiritual connection to all through spirit.

## Artha

The artha houses are 2, 6 and 10. They relate to the three earth signs (*earth triplicity*). The 2nd house relates to the first earth sign Taurus, the 6th Virgo and the 10th Capricorn. These houses define our material achievements, and the recognition gained from them. The 2nd house is about wealth and the material possessions gained. The 6th house is the urge to improve through hard work. The 10th house is the public recognition received through a career.

## Kama

The kama houses are 3, 7 and 11. They relate to the three air signs (*air triplicity*). The 3rd house relates to the first air sign Gemini, the 7th Libra, and the 11th Aquarius. These houses define how we convey our ideas, needs, and desires through relationships. The 3rd house describes our early relationships in which we learn by sharing with our siblings. The 7th house is the need of a lifelong partnership. The 11th house is the desire to feel connected to friends and groups or organizations.

## Moksha

The moksha houses are 4, 8 and 12. They relate to the three water signs (*water triplicity*). The 4$^{th}$ house relates to the first water sign Cancer, the 8$^{th}$ Scorpio, and the 12$^{th}$ Pisces.

Of all the aims of life, moksha is the ultimate goal. These are the houses that liberate or free the soul of the chains of earthly karma. They deal with the past, with our fear-based emotions, and the essence of the soul. The 4$^{th}$ house is the fear of losing our sense of security. The 8$^{th}$ house is the fear of letting go of control. The 12$^{th}$ house is represents releasing all our attachments to the world.

The third and last component of each Aim of Life, the end of each triplicity, brings us to the ultimate meaning and finality of its essence. The 9$^{th}$ house is concerned with the final results of the dharma houses (purpose), our spiritual realizations. The 10$^{th}$ house is concerned with the final result of the artha houses (worldly success and recognition), our material pursuits in this world. The 11$^{th}$ house is concerned with the final result of the kama houses (desire and relationships), our connection through humanity. But the moksha houses are the deep side of our soul, that which we do not know or understand. They are the mystery of life. The last of the moksha houses is the 12$^{th}$ house. This in essence becomes the most important house of all because it deals with our final liberation from this world.

# Opposing Houses

The first six houses are below the horizon making them a more personal experience, while the last six houses are above the horizon making them more public. The opposing houses have qualities that are one and the same but at opposite extremes.

**1/7**: The 1$^{st}$ house is the self. The 7$^{th}$ house is the self-experienced through relationships.

**2/8**: The 2$^{nd}$ house is personal money and wealth. The 8$^{th}$ house is money you share, or receive through other people.

**3/9**: The 3$^{rd}$ house is lower education and short distance trips. The 9$^{th}$ house is higher education like college, and long distance trips.

**4/10**: The 4$^{th}$ house is our private personal life at home. The 10$^{th}$ house is our public life or career.

The 5th house is our own children. The 11th house is humanity or the ? of the world.

**6/12**: The 6th house is personal service. The 12th house is public service.

## The planets signs of strength and weakness

When looking at a chart the planets take on the quality of the houses and meanings they rule. This will be determined through the meanings of the houses. Furthermore the strength that the planets are capable of delivering the meanings of the houses will be determined through their strength through the signs. The sign of exaltation is strongest then the sign that they rule. The sign they are weak in are the signs of debilitation.

## Signs (Rulership)

| | |
|---|---|
| **Sun** | rules Leo |
| **Moon** | rules Cancer |
| **Mercury** | rules Gemini and Virgo |
| **Venus** | rules Taurus and Libra |
| **Mars** | rules Aries and Scorpio |
| **Jupiter** | rules Sagittarius and Pisces |
| **Saturn** | rules Capricorn and Aquarius |

## Strong and Weak Signs for the Planets:

*Exaltation* is the strongest Sign and

*Debilitation* is the Weakest Sign

## Exaltation /Debilitation

| | | |
|---|---|---|
| **Sun** | Aries/Libra | 10 degrees |
| **Moon** | Taurus/Scorpio | 3 degrees |
| **Mercury** | Virgo/Pisces | 15 degrees |
| **Venus** | Pisces/Virgo | 27 degrees |
| **Mars** | Capricorn/Cancer | 28 degrees |

| Jupiter | Cancer/Capricorn | 5 degrees |
| --- | --- | --- |
| Saturn | Libra/Aries | 20 degrees |

# Basic Meaning of the Planets

The *Karaka* means what that planet is the "indicator of".

## Sun

It is the Karaka for the father, and rules, physical body, ego, self-confidence, males, life force, energy, giving out energy, boss, and leader. The Sun is a malefic and it has the ability to burn up or outshine other planets, this phenomenon is called combustion. Because Mercury is always close to the Sun it is not combust. It is a powerful force and can sometimes represent too much energy and causes problems in certain houses it occupies.

## Moon

It is the karaka for the mother, and rules, the mind and intelligence, emotions, females, receiving energy, reflection, public or masses, and the past.

## Mercury

It is the karaka of young people. It is Intelligence as in the thinking process of the mind, wit and humor, youth, learning, education, talking and any form of communication, sales, and travels.

## Venus

It is karaka of the wife in a male's chart, and rules female energy, relationships, the power of attraction in love, creativity and arts of all kinds, luxuries, beauty, grace and charm. Jupiter brings wealth but Venus as a wealth-producing planet brings opulent wealth. It is the planet that rules peace and balance.

## Mars

It is the karaka for all siblings, but since it rules male energy it may indicate a brother over a sister. It rules energy, courage, competition, and ambition. As the planet of war and anger it can stir up arguments and passion. A strong Mars is essential for success in business. It is also the karaka for intelligence and real estate.

## Jupiter

It is the karaka for the husband in a female's chart and it is the karaka of children. It rules wisdom, teachers, grace and long distance travels. Jupiter expands and can indicate growth, but sometimes excess. Jupiter brings opportunities, wealth and freedom. It is the planet of optimism and fun.

## Saturn

Saturn is the karaka of the elderly and death. It rules old and historical things. Saturn will cause delays, setbacks but can indicate longevity. Saturn causes contraction while Jupiter is expansion. It rules structure, discipline, responsibility and endurance. Saturn is the great teacher through the wisdom of experience. The lessons learned are life lessons, which are usually through hard work and the hard knocks of life.

## Rahu

Rahu rules our intense desires that bring us into this life. It can rule addictions for it gives but with a price. It rules the extremes of life and problems, consequences and attachments to the materialistic world. It rules obsessions and compulsions. Rahu is the future while Ketu is the past.

## Ketu

Ketu is the karaka for the outcast in society, and is the spiritual side of life, ruling over other worldliness. It is the indicator of loss and indicates death. Rahu is what takes us into this material world through our desires and Ketu takes us out of this world. The house that Ketu occupies indicates a sense of something always missing, as a feeling of an emptiness or void. Trying to fill the empty void may be the obsessive focus throughout life.

# Bhavat Bhavam

# House to House

*All I have seen teaches me to trust the creator for all I have not seen.*

*Ralph Waldo Emerson 1803-1882*

***Bhavat bhavam*** is a Sanskrit phrase that means "*from house to house*". In Western astrology this is known as derivative houses. Here you will learn to utilize the basic meaning of the houses and apply them in relationship to each. For example, the basic meaning of the 2nd house is wealth, and money. Therefore the 2nd house in numerical order to any of the houses will indicate the wealth or money acquired from that house. The 2nd house to the 7th house (which is the 8th house) will indicate the wealth and money of the spouse (7th house); the 2nd house to the 5th house (6th house) will indicate the financial prosperity of the children (5th house), and the 2nd house to the 10th house (11th house) will indicate financial gain through the career (10th house). And so on.

When counting from the house to house you must count the house you are beginning with as number one. So in counting the 2nd house from the 7th you must count the 7th house as first and the 8th house as second, and so the 8th house is the 2nd house from the 7th house.

The 12th house to any house indicates the end or final outcome to whatever the house in question represents. For example, the 6th house is the 12th to the 7th (marriage), so it represents the end of the marriage. The 3rd house is the end of the parents because it is the 12th to the 4th (parents).

The maraka houses derive their meaning from this exact principle. The maraka houses are the 2nd and 7th houses and are called the "killer houses". Since the 3rd house is our energy, will, and life force and the 12th house is the house of loss, then the 2nd house is the loss of our life force. It is the 12th from the 3rd. Similarly the 8th house is our length of life so the 12th from the

8th (7th house) would be the loss of life. Death of the mother is the 11th house because it is the 8th from the 4th (mother). Death of the father is the 4th house because it is the 8th from the 9th (father). The planets that rule the maraka houses are the maraka planets.

Grandchildren are the 9th house, because they are our children's children, 5th from the 5th. Maternal aunts and uncles are the 6th house because they would be the 3rd house (siblings) from the 4th (mother). Paternal aunts and uncles are the 11th house because they are the 3rd (siblings) from the 9th (father). The maternal grandmother would be the 7th house, the mother's mother, the 4th from the 4th. The paternal grandmother would be the 12th house because this house is the 4th (mother) from the 9th (father).

In the case of twins that are born minutes apart with birth charts almost the same you would differentiate them by looking at the 3rd house as the younger sibling, and the 11th house as the elder sibling. In the elder twin's chart, the 3rd house would describe the younger twin and in the younger twin's chart the 11th house would describe the elder twin.

Let's say someone asks you about the health of their youngest brother's wife, because she is ill. You would look to the 3rd house (youngest brother) count seven houses (wife) from the 3rd house and arrive at the 9th house. You would then count six houses (health, illness) from the 9th house and arrive at the 2nd house. The planets in the 2nd house and the transits aspecting this house will reveal the answers.

Any family relatives and their situations can be assessed through rotating the chart to the appropriate house and taking it as the ascendant. To read your spouse you would take the 7th house of your chart, rotate it so as to become the ascendant and take the entire chart as the spouse's chart. In other words the 7th house becomes the 1st house. You will be able to determine all the areas of life relating to your spouse in this way. The 9th house would be the ascendant to be read as your father's chart. The 4th house would become the ascendant for your mother. As another example, say you have three brothers and you are number two in the birth order of four boys. How do you assess which house is which brother?

The 3rd house is generally for the well being of all siblings, but we know we have quite different relationships with each of them. There are also differences in their individual lives. The 3rd house would be counted as the 1st house for the youngest brother, and the 3rd from the 3rd (5th house) would be the brother or sister before the youngest. You would keep counting three houses away from the previous one for each younger sibling, going from youngest to older until you reach your place in the birth order. The 11th house is the eldest sibling. If you had two brothers or sisters who were both older than you, the 11th house would represent the eldest, and counting three houses from the 11th (1st house) would be the one born after the oldest sibling.

To read your own children in a chart, the first-born would be the 5th house, and the second born would be the 3rd from the 5th (brother or sister to the first born). Each child would be counted three houses from the previous one. So the third born would be the 3rd house from the 7th, which is the 9th house. The house referring to each particular child can be looked at as their ascendant. The entire chart (all twelve houses) becomes their chart using the ascendant arrived at for their 1st house. Thus, reading it as their individual chart. The transits and dashas will reveal more of their current situations.

In the case of first, second and third marriages or spouses, I have not found a particular system for this to work, maybe because divorce is not an option in India. Some say you look to the 3rd from the 7th (9th house) for the second marriage, and continue counting on three houses for each marriage. Personally I believe the 7th house will always reveal the current marriage. Even though the person we are married to may change, it is still our current marriage and we only have one marriage partner at a time. Again the future dashas and transits will reveal the differences in the partners.

In the texts the principle of "*Bhavat Bhavam*" states that the number of the house from the lagna when counted again the same number of houses will give additional information pertaining to the original house. In other words, the 2nd house from the 2nd house is the 3rd house; the 3rd from the 3rd is the 5th and so on. For example, the 4th house from the ascendant rules the mother. Therefore, the 4th house from the 4th house (7th house) would be as relevant to the mother as the 4th house. The 9th house from the 9th house (5th house) will reveal more information about the father.

Ironically, in both examples, the house arrived at ($7^{th}$ – $4^{th}$ from the $4^{th}$), ($5^{th}$ – $9^{th}$ from the $9^{th}$) are the mother's mother, and the father's father. The $8^{th}$ house from the $8^{th}$ house becomes the $3^{rd}$ house, giving the $3^{rd}$ house death inflicting qualities. What seems to happen is a perpetuation of each house by this sort of numerical duplication. The $6^{th}$ house from the $6^{th}$ house is the $11^{th}$ house. The $11^{th}$ house can reveal the result of illness and healing, or your enemy's enemy (your friend).

Each house has specific meanings and these divisions will determine all the areas of our lives. To look at these meanings and then relate them to each other is referred to as *Bhavat Bhavam*, meaning from house to house. The numerical value will carry the meanings of the numbered houses. For example, the $1^{st}$ house will always refer to the physical form of the individual. Therefore, the number one will always be that person, and house number two will always refer to acquisition as with finances and money. The application of the meanings of the houses to one another actually shows how everything in the chart as well as in life is interrelated. This is actually the mathematics of the universe, how everything is connected. As we go through all the meanings of the houses and inter-relate them, you will start to understand the perfection and profound depth of this divine science.

## Mystery of Numbers

What comes alive is the numerological meanings and how these are applied on to themselves. Numbers seem to make more sense as their relationship and meanings are applied. Mathematical patterns seem to emerge giving order to this divine puzzle, thus, giving more understanding to life's puzzle. Here we see the mechanics of the universe.

There are 12 houses and the number 12 seems to be the mystical number of completion. The 12 houses cover all the experiences of life. There are 12 zodiacal signs, 12 apostles representing the 12 personalities of the signs. Also, there are 12 energy centers in the body represented by the chakras that control the hormonal functions in the body. There are 12 dimensions. The $12^{th}$ dimension is oneness with God. It is said to be inconceivable to the human mind. As we progress through life it is a progression through the 12 houses that represents our growth from the beginning to the end of life. Three is devisable into twelve, four times. There are four elements - fire, earth, air and water.

Additionally, there are three qualities cardinal, fixed and mutable. There are three qualities and four elements, three times four equals 12. These are the variables of the numerical values that give the signs, houses and planets meaning. We use nine planets in Vedic astrology. This includes the planets visible to the naked eye, Mercury, Venus, Mars, Jupiter and Saturn, the Sun and Moon plus the lunar nodes, Rahu and Ketu. If we added the three outer planets Uranus, Neptune and Pluto we complete the picture of 12 planets.

Because these planets are invisible to the naked eye their energies are unclear to our conscious awareness. But no doubt, do affect us on a deep level. I believe they affect the mass consciousness. As we develop and grow in higher consciousness we begin to tap into this energy, which is profoundly powerful and metaphysical. But as it is now, they motivate us in unconscious and usually negative behaviors. Our reactions on an unconscious level are based on our unconscious fears. With conscious understanding of our fears we can conquer our most negative behaviors that seem like obsessions, compulsions and addictions. The outer planets are the keys to this.

## Power of Three

In numerology, if you add the individual numbers of the number 12 together, one plus two equals three. As you know three is an extremely mystical number. This has been demonstrated over time.

When we arrive at the number three we start to see the repetitive powers. This is why three is such powerful and mystical number. Let me demonstrate what I mean by the repetitive powers. Starting with the 3rd house I will continue around the chart each time counting three houses from the previous one. Starting with the 3rd house itself, it is the 2nd from the 2nd and the 8th from the 8th. And, continues when counting three houses away from the 3rd house. As in the 5th house is the 3rd from the 3rd and the 9th from the 9th. The 7th house is the 10th from the 10th and the 4th from the 4th. The 9th house is the 5th from the 5th and the 11th from the 11th. The 11th house is the 6th from the 6th and the 12th from the 12th. And of course the 1st house is the 1st from the 1st and the 7th from the 7th. This is the pattern counting three houses away from each other starting with the 3rd house in any chart.

# The Trine within the Four Elements

## Four Aims of Life

The triangle is a very mystical symbol; the pyramids of ancient Egypt themselves are built in this shape. A triangle has three equal sides, and the number 3 may be regarded as a symbol of completion. The number 3 appears throughout history in many cultures and religions. There are, for example, the three worlds or three levels of consciousness: consciousness, unconsciousness, and cosmic consciousness. Western psychology may define these same three worlds as the ego, the shadow, and the self. In the Vedanta philosophy of India, the three gunas are the ingredients of the nature of matter:

| | |
|---|---|
| Sattva | goodness and virtue |
| Rajas | passion and desire |
| Tamas | darkness or ignorance |

The three gunas are in varying degrees in all beings of matter.

In Christianity the number 3 is exemplified by way of the Holy Trinity. This concept suggests that three apparent gods are in fact one and the same thing. This would seem, once again, to be our eternal triad of body, mind, and spirit. God the Son is the body, God the Father the mind, and God the Holy Ghost is the spirit. These constitute the whole person.

It is said that things happen in threes. When a major world event occurs, we can expect it to happen two more times. Plane crashes occur this way, and so do other major events. On a personal level, I know that when something comes up for me three times, it's definite. It's like baseball - three strikes and you're out.

In astrology the number 3 gives order and meaning to this symbolic system of self-discovery. Astrology has four elements, but there are three signs that comprise each of these elements. There are three fire signs, three earth signs, three air signs, and three water signs. These signs form triangles to each other in the birth chart. This is what is referred to as the trine aspect. In a 360-degree circle each element of the same quality is 120 degrees away from the other or 5 signs away. This relationship is 1, 5, and 9.

According to Vedic philosophy there are four aims of life. These four aims are part of the integrated human experience. The four aims of life are **dharma**, **artha**, **kama**, and **moksha**, and they are related to the four elements. From this perspective the meanings of the four elements take on much deeper meanings, and help us understand the life process. This deeper understanding can help us see life as a progression to higher consciousness. As we delve into the trinity of these four aims we come to understand the illusion of it all.

The realization of the illusion of the material plane brings us to enlightenment. Nothing really matters in the end except that all these experiences lead us to the one and only realization that releasing all desire and attachment to this world gives our final liberation, which is moksha.

When we become enlightened to this truth, we realize that moksha is the highest level. Until we learn what is real and truly lasting, there will always be suffering. If it isn't immortal, then it isn't real. The only immortal part of our selves is our soul. Moksha is what frees and liberates our soul from maya (illusion). We will come to understand this fourth dimension as we journey through life, and experience healing from the triangle within these four elements or four aims of life.

The trine is the aspect of healing. It is the aspect that gives ease and flow. In astrology, the four elements fire, earth, air and water all trine each other. They work in unison with each other.

# Part I

# Fire Triplicity – Dharma Houses
## 1ˢᵗ House, 5ᵗʰ House and 9ᵗʰ House

*Without the spiritual world the material world is a disheartening enigma.*

*Joseph Joubert 1754-1824*

## Dharma

The fire element corresponds to our dharma, and dharma is our sense of purpose. When we understand our purpose, we are connected to our spirit and guided by inspiration. The spirit is what fuels our life. The dharma houses are 1, 5, and 9. As with all the other elements, these fire houses trine each other.

Aries is the first sign of the natural zodiac; it is also the first fire sign, followed by Leo, then Sagittarius. These three signs are called the *fire triplicity*. They are 1, 5, and 9 in relationship to one another. The 1ˢᵗ, 5ᵗʰ, and 9ᵗʰ houses are therefore the houses relating to fire or dharma.

The dharma houses 1, 5, and 9 and the fire signs relate to our spirit. The 1ˢᵗ house is the beginning of life. Aries represents new beginnings. The 1ˢᵗ house/first sign Aries is the development of the self (our sense of who we are), our outward show to the world. It is how others see us, and it is the house of our self-image. It is our beginning into this world. Our life force and physical body are determined here, and the life force is our vitality itself.

The self needs to extend itself beyond the self and this is done through the creative process. Spirit comes out through the process of creativity. It feels its sense of purpose through self-expression.

True creative expression is the outpouring of the inner spirit expressing itself in the outer world. This is inspiration.

The 5th house of the horoscope as well as the fifth sign Leo is where this outward flow of energy manifests through creativity. This is how spirit moves us, and we move others through extending our spirit in our own creative expressions.

The 9th house and ninth sign Sagittarius symbolizes how we believe. It holds our spiritual beliefs and truths. The 9th house gives us an understanding of what our spirit is. Spirit is the spark of life that unites us. It is the non-personal force that abides in all-living beings. It is our connection to the eternal divine oneness. We are all parts of this one cosmic God.

Therefore the process of spirit is:

- the manifestation of the spirit in the body as the life force (1st house),
- the need of spirit to extend itself through creative expression (5th house), and
- the *true* expression of spirit, which comes when we realize we *are* spirit (9th house).

This how the fire triplicity works. When we feel spirit working through us, we are connected to our purpose in life. All human beings are born with an innate desire to know their purpose in life, in order to give their life meaning. The spiritual triangle does just that. It gives us our sense of purpose – hence these are the dharma houses.

# The 1st House: Birth of the Self

*Life's experiences are intended to make you eventually face yourself.*
*Face reality!*

*Harold Sherman*

**Thanu Bhava:** Physical body, stature of body, limbs of the body, constitution, ego, personality, appearance, self, character, entrance into the world, birth, head.

### Kendra, Trikona, Dharma

## The 1st house extends through all the other Houses or Life's Experiences

The 1st house extends its hands through all the other houses as it manifest through all these other life experiences. It doesn't have as much meaning as the other houses because it expresses itself through the energies, and meanings of these other life's experiences, which the 1st house plays through these other houses. It is actually the experience of the individual, self (1st house) through life (all the other houses). So the self or the 1st house is lived through the other houses. This is the person's evolution through life or the process of living life through life's experiences.

## The Most Important House in a Chart

The 1st house is considered the most important house of the chart for no other houses could exist without the 1st house initiating the entire horoscope. It is the house of the individual and is the beginning of life and entrance into the world. It sets up the entire chart and depending on the sign that is rising on the Eastern horizon at the time of birth determines the entire life experiences, and who the person is.

## Beginning of Life

At the time of birth when the infant comes into this world it is the time of the first breath that initiates the beginning as a separate entity from the mother and starts the beginning of life. So the exact time of the first breath is the time the birth chart is erected. The sign and degree on the eastern horizon is the degree and sign calculated for the ascendant and 1$^{st}$ house. The proceeding houses of the horoscope follow in their natural order of the zodiac.

So if Aries is the rising sign at the time of birth then Taurus is on the 2$^{nd}$ house, Gemini on the 3$^{rd}$, Cancer on the 4$^{th}$, Leo on the 5$^{th}$, Virgo in the 6$^{th}$, Libra, on the 7$^{th}$, Scorpio on the 8$^{th}$, Sagittarius on the 9$^{th}$, Capricorn on the 10$^{th}$, Aquarius on the 11$^{th}$, and Pisces on the 12$^{th}$. This is the natural order of the zodiac. If Scorpio were rising on the Ascendant then the 2$^{nd}$ house would be Sagittarius because it is the sign that naturally follows Scorpio and the sequential natural order follows all the 12 signs through to the 12$^{th}$ house.

## The Houses are a Stage

The houses are the area of life that we all process and experience in a lifetime. They can be seen as the cycle of life's process as we evolve or grow through life. All areas of life fall into a house. The houses are stages that life will unfold. The planets are the energy but the houses are the areas of our life that this activity will take place. While the signs are the qualities that the planet will express, their powers are derived by the sign the planets are placed in.

## Planets Carry the Meanings of the Houses

The sign on the 1$^{st}$ house will determine the entire order as to what planets rule each house. The planets carry the meanings of the houses they rule so this determines which planets are good or bad for a chart. It gives an entire set up of what planets are strong or weak for a chart.

Once the ascendant is determined by the birth time then the signs on each house will determine where the planets are to be in each of the houses, depending on where the planets are at the time of birth. Each planet is placed in the houses ruling the sign that each planet is in at birth. If the Sun is in Scorpio and the 8$^{th}$ house contains the sign Scorpio then the Sun is placed in the 8$^{th}$ house.

## 1st House determines the entire Setup of a Chart

So the 1st house is the house that determines the entire set up for a chart. It will concern the person's entire physical make up, such as the way a person looks, their personality and physical health. It is how the world views or sees them. The sign or planets in this house will add to the color or expression you extend outward to the world.

## The Birthing Process

The 1st house is our entrance into this world meaning that it indicates the entire process and circumstances involved in the birthing process. Either an easy or difficult birth will be reflected in the 1st house. Malefic planets in the 1st house can indicate a difficult birth and sometimes Mars can indicate a caesarian birth, since Mars rules knives and cutting. Ketu on the ascendant can represent a very difficult birth, or even near death experience.

The 1st house rules the head as in the very top of the body and it is no accident that humans are normally born headfirst. The sign Aries is the 1st sign in the natural zodiac and pertains to new beginnings. This can indicate the birth of anything and initiates a brand new start and fresh beginning. The individual will come out with a clean new slate.

The 1st house is the initial start of life as to the entire circumstances into this world. It can indicate the family and parents. It actually reflects the entire chart and life we are born into, for the 1st house sets up the entire life and directs where all the planets will be placed in the chart directing the enfoldment of life.

## Physical Body

The 1st house determines the physical body and stature, and the physical stamina and health. The physical health can be determined by the 1st house., It is also the ego and reflects self-esteem. It is the sense of who they believe they are at a deep core level.

It determines certain physical appearances, such as height, weight, complexion and type of hair.

## New Beginnings

And in the cycle of life as planets continue to move through the horoscope as the planets continue to transit in the heavens, their entrance into the 1st house brings new beginnings into life throughout the lifetime.

## Kendra and Trikona

As a Kendra house (angle) it is one of the areas of importance indicating power and strength in an individual. But the fact that it is also a Trikona indicates this is one of the houses that is a part of the inspiration that is a driving force in life. They are driven to aspire to what they came to be in the world. This is the 1$^{st}$ house. The qualities of the 1$^{st}$ house is what they aspire to be and directs the interest throughout life.

## Dharma House

As a Dharma house this connects this house to the fiery nature of Aries, which is where they initiate the being of who and what they are. Planets in the 1$^{st}$ house are strong, dynamic and powerful. The individual feels a sense of their dharma and purpose and strives to be what they have come to this world to do and be. This house can determine to a great extent the fate and destiny. Important planets in this house will have a definite mark on the lives of these individuals.

# Bhavat Bhavam

## The First House

**It is the 1$^{st}$ from the 1st.** The core meaning of the 1st house is our physical entrance into the world and represents our physical constitution and personality we present to the world. It is the new beginning, start of life and consequently our birth into this world. I am that I am. The body part is the head. Incidentally, we are generally born into this world headfirst.

**It is the 7$^{th}$ from the 7$^{th}$ house.** This means the partner's partner. Therefore, it represents how the partner's will view the individual in relationship. Relationships are seen from their viewpoint. This is the validation from others in intimate relationships.

**It is the 2$^{nd}$ from the 12$^{th}$ house.** This indicates gains through loss. For the 2$^{nd}$ house is always acquisition of whatever the house in reference is about, and here it is referring to the 12$^{th}$. Therefore, it is what is gained or acquired from loss. This is a new life. For the 12$^{th}$ house to any house is loss or endings pertaining to the house in reference. The 12$^{th}$ house in the natal chart is the last and final house, so it is the end of life, and what else can be gained through the end of life but a new life or new incarnation.

Another indication for the 12$^{th}$ house is expenditures and the 1$^{st}$ house can mean financial expenditures being the 12$^{th}$ from the 2$^{nd}$ as in expenditures in start up costs in new ventures.

**It is the 12$^{th}$ from the 2$^{nd}$ house**. This indicates the power of speech, the end result of our speech. It can be the house of financial loss, expenditures from new projects or beginnings. It can represent independence, going out alone or loss of early childhood.

**It is the 3$^{rd}$ from the 11$^{th}$ house**. This is the younger sibling to the eldest sibling. The next eldest in the birth order if one has siblings older. The 11$^{th}$ house is the eldest sibling; the next eldest would be the 1$^{st}$ house counting three houses away. If there are more that are older (siblings) then continue counting three houses away from the previous house. This house describes the will, courage, artistic talents, communication skills and travel potential of the eldest sibling. It is the ability to convey desires or goals in life, and the amount of courage to pursue goals or dreams. It is striving to attain desires and to communicate with friends.

**It is the 11$^{th}$ from the 3$^{rd}$ house**. The 11$^{th}$ house is desires and gains and the 3$^{rd}$ is the communicative skills and will power therefore, the 1$^{st}$ house will indicate the power to achieve goals. It indicates the sibling's friends and desires, particularly the youngest sibling's friends. It is the ultimate goals and competitive force to achieve.

**It is the 4$^{th}$ from the 10$^{th}$ house**. This confers a sense of security from the social standing. It is how one feels based on how their image is viewed by the public. Therefore, it is the personal image as viewed by others thus referring to the personality.

**It is the 10$^{th}$ from the 4$^{th}$ house**. This is a kendra (angle) from a kendra, and the 1$^{st}$ house is a kendra, so this gives it double power. It is what they develop into from the sense of who they are based on the feelings of security. If they are given a firm foundation and feel protected they can grow into powerful and confident people. This will affect the ability to achieve great positions in the world. Sometimes the sense of fear motivates. But fear as the motivator can bring out unconscious negative behavior patterns. The 4$^{th}$ house is the sense of security and the 10$^{th}$ is achievements therefore, the 1$^{st}$ will represent confidence and ability to achieve goals as in a career or social standing.

**It is the 5th from the 9th house.** It is the father's children, therefore represents the individual, and how the father sees them. It is the creative mind of the father or teacher. It is what they believe about themselves.

**It is the 9th from the 5th house.** It is the children's beliefs or spirituality. It is their beliefs in themselves. It is the belief of who they are and their own truths.

**It is the 6th from the 8th house.** The 1st house has always meant injury to the physical body when difficult planets are placed here. The 6th house is accidents and the 8th house can indicate death. It can also indicate how healthy the physical body is and the constitution.

**It is the 8th from the 6th house.** Since the 8th house is the house of change and transformations, this can mean changes in a health regime to improve the health. It is the physical changes that they manifest because of self-improvement. But it can indicate death due to injury.

Since the 1st house can indicate health and physical stamina. Planets in this house can either give strength or health problems. Regardless if the planet is a natural benefic or malefic the houses the planet rules will determine the ability the planet has to give health problems. Generally planets that rule the Dusthana houses, 6, 8 or 12 can bring health issues. Also planets that rule the 11th house can cause health problems when placed in the 1st house.

# Planets in the 1st House

## Sun

The Sun is the life force of our planet. It is the soul and spirit of a chart. However it can be an overpowering influence. If it is too close to other planets it can burn up their capability to function properly. This condition is called combustion of the Sun. Its forceful presence can be excessive and cause problems.

The Sun in the 1st house can give a powerful sense of the self but can be overwhelming. It is hard to consider how others may be feeling for the power of the self will be the first inclination. There can be a selfish attitude but the individual doesn't realize till it may be brought to their attention. They feel the world revolves around them. They have a strong self-esteem and are egocentric. They take command and are in power in many aspects of their life. This is a powerful placement but consideration for others must be practiced. They may be the 1ˢᵗ born in their family needing to be first in everything. They are very competitive for they need to be number one. The Sun can burn the head in the 1ˢᵗ house causing baldness. The Sun in Leo or Aries will intensify the Sun's energy here.

## Moon

Moon in the 1ˢᵗ house can cause a great amount of sensitivity overacting to the feeling senses. They feel and sense everything in the environment intensely, such as sounds, smells, lights, colors, and also pick up on the feelings of others, like an emotional sponge. Crowded areas feel weird and confused due to the bombardment of many people and their feelings. The home is a refuge from the world. Places by the water are desired, and baths are healing and comforting. The life has many unpredictable turns and events with constant changes in their daily activities. The Moon in Cancer can exaggerate all these qualities all the more.

## Mercury

Mercury in the 1ˢᵗ house gives the capacity to learn and process information constantly. All forms of communication are a big part of their life. Conversations and connecting to people are important. The phone bills are high. They are great with words spoken or written, and fantastic conversational speakers. A sense of humor keeps them jovial and fun to be with. Always youthful in their actions they always look way younger than their years. Travel and exploration of the world keeps them moving. Interested in many areas of life they are never bored. Mercury in Gemini and Virgo will give the best of Mercury's qualities in this person's life.

## Venus

Venus in the 1ˢᵗ house gives charm, grace and beauty. Social graces are one of their gifts. They need others to feel connected and balanced; relationships are a big part of their life. They have the need to be surrounded by beauty and art. They appreciate the arts and enjoy participation in areas that support and develop artistic pursuits. This placement can denote a certain amount of luck and fortune. Venus in Libra or Taurus will accentuate these qualities intensely. Venus in Pisces in the 1ˢᵗ house will bring sensuality but with health issues.

## Mars

Mars in the first gives energy, drive, ambition and a competitive edge. Shining Mars is called the "bright one" and in the 1st house one shines and stands out in a crowd. Their intelligence is strong and powerful but their athletic ability usually outweighs the mental powers. A beautiful head of hair is common with waves or curls surrounding the face. They can never sit still always in a state of motion, impulsive and in a hurry moving fast all the time. Because of the constant state of action they are sometimes nervous and reckless. They are prone to accidents and the place of injury appears to the head. The blood flow to the head can be a problem, as they are prone to headaches or stokes.

## Jupiter

An optimistic and jovial nature exudes from this placement, always seeing the glass as half full instead of half empty. They are well intentioned and happy. But have to have others see it their way. Their truths are the absolute way. They can be overly zealous being an authority and feel the need to teach and lead others particularly in their beliefs. They tend to exaggerate because the 1st house is the physical body they may be overweight particularly if the sign on the ascendant is water, Cancer, Scorpio or Pisces. They are inspirational and compassionate especially when others accept their ways of living.

## Saturn

Saturn indicates a strong sense of responsibility. They are born old souls and never really have the opportunity to be children. They somehow feel responsible for everyone. They take care of their parents and other family members. There may be a difficult circumstance surrounding their birth or family.

Their sense of responsibility gives them great capacity to organize and structure many areas of life. They lead and direct in many organizations. They need to care for others to feel their sense of importance. They are determined, with a great sense of responsibility, never letting others down they are dependable, reliable and always on time. They may start out slow, but with endurance they are always the ones who make it to the finish line. They tend to worry too much and can age prematurely.

## Rahu

Rahu in the 1ˢᵗ house gives a sense of importance, as it is a powerful placement for a life of intensity. This gives a life of fate and destiny. As they plan for the future it seems events just sweep them off into another direction always putting them on the correct course even though it is the exact opposite of the original plan. People and events are extreme. The world is an adventure of the unknown and uncharted territory that they will experience unplanned. Things just seem to happen out of the blue. Physically they can be robust and sometimes larger than life, literally and figuratively. Circumstances involving the materialistic world consume peace of mind and cause many upsets throughout life. Attachments to a world of money and superficiality can destroy their world. But with Ketu in the 7ᵗʰ house their partners take up a vast amount of energy and time. Steer clear of victims in relationships, they can drain your energy and time. Many times the partner has bright or very light colored eyes.

## Ketu

Ketu in the 1ˢᵗ gives a very elusive quality and the feeling of being very hard to understand or know. There is one foot in reality and one foot out, connected to a vast spiritual world. They are unconnected at times feeling unsupported and feeling like they don't fit in anywhere. There is a sense of disconnection, and alienation wanting to escape to another world or place. Many times the body can be very thin especially in the younger years.

Rahu will be in the 7ᵗʰ indicating a partner who is very materialistic and bigger than life, causing great concern and problems in marriage.

# Ruler of the 1ˢᵗ House in Various Houses

The ruling planet of the 1ˢᵗ house is the ruler of the chart therefore the house this very important planet resides in is of utmost importance. This house will of major importance and interest throughout the life of the individual.

## 1ˢᵗ House

The ruler of the 1ˢᵗ house in the 1ˢᵗ house focuses the person on matters in their personal environment. They will be very self-consumed and not able to see outside of their own world. The individual may not venture far from home and sees things through a veil of conditions and personal beliefs.

## 2nd House

The ruler of the 1st in the 2nd house. Money matters are a major focus throughout life. There is a strong sense of self-esteem and a drive to improve one's position in life through financial achievements.

## 3rd House

A strong courageous drive empowers the individual for success. Ambition in competitive fields builds a strong and powerful body. Athletic strength directs the individual into sports or dance. Creative expression comes through communications such as writing.

## 4th House

Love of home and a desire to connect to the family is one of the most important aspects of life. There is an interest in real estate, home design, or construction. The mother is important throughout life.

## 5th House

There is a powerful need for self-expression. The arts or any form of creativity may be an outlet for this individual's inspiration. Children will be an important part of their life. They are good at speculation such as investing in the stock market.

## 6th House

Hard work, diligence, and respect for discipline give this individual their strength of character. They work hard and long hours. Health is important and they are concerned with their diet and exercise. They desire to help others in a line of service to humanity.

## 7th House

Relationships are extremely important and they give most of their time to helping their partner and improving their relationship. They tend to lose a sense of the self in their relationships always sacrificing their needs for others.

## 8th House

Life can be a struggle especially in early life. Poor health or lack of drive through early hardship builds character. There is an interest in metaphysical studies as there is an interest in things beyond this world.

## 9<sup>th</sup> House

Spirituality and philosophical studies are a major interest throughout lift. Travel and interest in worldly matters on a global level directs their life. The father can be a powerful influence.

## 10<sup>th</sup> House

Career and social position is the main focus throughout life. There is a driving force to climb to the top of the chosen field of work. Attention and possible fame may come from the drive and ambition to be the best.

## 11<sup>th</sup> House

Social events involving influential people and connections will direct the life in a positive way. Interest in humanitarian efforts will be a focus in life. Friends give support and comfort throughout life.

## 12<sup>th</sup> House

Privacy and solitude is essential to regain and build balance and wholeness in personal awareness. Early life is difficult and the individual stays out of public attention. They can be reclusive and shy as children.

*Sri Sathya Sai Baba* was an Indian Guru who was considered to be an avatar and saint by his follows. He was reported to have mystical powers where he was able to materialize objects out of thin air and there were many reports of miraculous healings.

| 5th h. 24 | | 6th h. 35 | | 7th h. 20 | | 8th h. 25 | |
|---|---|---|---|---|---|---|---|
| ♅ᴿ 02:45 PBh | ♓ | ♂ᴿ 13:02 Ash | ♈ | | ♉ | ☊☌ 14:47 Ard<br>☽ 19:06 Ard<br>♀ᴿ 22:51 Pun | ♊ |
| 4th h. 27 | ♒ | Sri Sathya Sai Baba<br>Tue 11-23-1926<br>06:22:00<br>Puttapaka, Andhra Pradesh<br>India<br>Timezone: -5:30:00 DST: 0<br>Latitude: 17N06'00<br>Longitude: 78E56'00<br>Ayanamsha : -22:49:51 Lahiri | | | | | ♋ 9th h. 27 |
| ♃ 27:01 Dha | ♑ 3rd h. 30 | | | | | ♆ 04:08 Mag | ♌ 10th h. 35 |
| ☋ 14:47 PSh | ♐ | ♄05:59 Anu<br>☿06:09 Anu<br>☉07:08 Anu<br>♀07:31 Anu<br>☿ᴿ14:00 Anu | ♍ | | ♎ | | ♏ |
| 2nd h. 22 | | 1st h. 32 | | 12th h. 20 | | 11th h. 46 | |

*Chart 1: Sri Sathya Sai Baba*

He was revered by many but he did have a bit of controversy and skeptics believed he was a fraud. He later had accusations of sexual abuses. Nonetheless, many claimed he helped them grow and revered him as a mystical spiritual teacher with great powers.

Sai Baba has four planets in the 1st house in Scorpio. He has Saturn, Sun, Venus and Mercury. The Sun will make him self-serving but with Saturn there is a quality of self-sacrifice and discipline to serve others. The Sun rules the 10th house of social standing, fame and work so he is well know known for his work and service. Venus is the same degree as the Sun producing the power of attraction. In the sign of Scorpio he is very magnetic and passionate about what he does. As Venus rules the 7th and 12th houses he connects himself with partners that help him with his spiritual pursuits. As Mercury is ruler of the 8th and the 11th houses this brings his quality of magnetism to large groups of people. Saturn grounds his teachings and rulership as a guru of deep spiritual knowledge for it rules the 3rd house of teaching and the 4th house of home.

*Grace Kelly* was a beautiful actress with perfect features from the glamorous Hollywood era. Prince Rainier III of Monaco asked to marry her for she was the epitome of sophistication, grace, charm and beauty.

| 6th h. 36 | 7th h. 24 | 8th h. 23 | 9th h. 24 |
|---|---|---|---|
| ♅℞ 15:04 UBh | ☊ 19:17 Bha | ♃℞ 21:13 Roh | ♀℞ 26:39 Pun |
| ☽ 28:58 PBh | Grace Kelly<br>Tue 11-12-1929<br>05:31:00<br>Philadelphia, PA,Pennsylvania<br>USA<br>Timezone: 5 DST: 0<br>Latitude: 39N57'08<br>Longitude: 75W09'51<br>Ayanamsha : -22:52:26 Lahiri | | |
| | | ♇ 10:32 Mag | |
| ♄ 05:13 Mul | ♂ 02:45 Vis | ☿ 05:58 Cht<br>℞ 11:49 Swa<br>♀ 17:49 Swa<br>♆ 19:17 Swa<br>☉ 26:41 Vis | |
| 3rd h. 35 | 2nd h. 20 | 1st h. 27 | 12th h. 25 |

*Chart 2: Grace Kelly*

To better understand the 1st house Grace Kelly's chart exemplifies the power of planets placed here. She has Venus the plant of beauty, grace and charm in the 1st house in the powerful sign Libra. This is the ruler of the 1st house in the first house, fortifying this house with the powers of planet Venus. This makes the essence of Venus shine. Grace was known for her perfect sophisticated beauty and all the qualities of Venus because the 1st house is the physical body.

Venus represents the arts and she was very creative and an accomplished award winning actress. Venus also rules luxuries and she was born into a wealthy family in Philadelphia but then became the Princess of Monaco one the richest countries in the world where she lived a life of opulence and royalty. As Venus rules the 8th house it brings a quality of charisma to her appearance for the 8th house gives the power of attraction.

Mercury in the 1$^{st}$ house gives her the power to communicate and delegate pleasingly in the sign of Libra. Mercury rules the 9$^{th}$ and 12$^{th}$ houses, which pertain to foreign lands and travel. She was brought to live in another country. Both Venus and Mercury benefic planets in her chart are with Ketu, which turns the energy of Ketu positive. When a benefic is conjunct Ketu and its own sign of rulership, as Venus it empowers the house incredibly. This may be why her life was so notable and significant from a top Hollywood movie star to the Princess of Monaco.

The Sun in the 1$^{st}$ house can indicate a self centered attitude which was probably the case in her acting years but since the Sun is debilitated and conjunct Ketu she had to give up her career in Hollywood and surrender her life to serve as a Princess. The Sun rules the 11$^{th}$ house of wealth and her life was of extreme opulence.

# The 5th House: Inspiration of Creative Expression

*"Your visions will become clear only when you can look into your own heart. Who looks outside, dreams; who looks inside, awakes."*

*Carl G Jung*

**Putra Bhava.** True intelligence, the mind, children, abortions, creativity, good karma received in this lifetime (poorva-punya), sense of destiny, ability to see the future, morals, pleasure, romance, fun, speculation, lotteries, entertainment, sports, generosity, spiritual rituals, kings or politics, advisor, heart.

### Trikona, Dharma

### Opening the Heart

When we extend our heart outside of our selves we feel an opening that gives a deep sense of pleasure. This is the sense of opening your heart. All 5th house matters open the heart. Having children opens the heart; a part of you extends outward through your creation and love. The sense of self is extended beyond oneself. Having children is a selfless act.

### Talent

The 5th house is talent. This involves creativity and the mental process that is involved in being creative. When one has a natural aptitude to be good at something they are inspired to work more with the encouragement from others.

### Fun and Entertainment

The 5th house is the house of fun and entertainment. The energy that exudes from someone in a mental framework of fun and excitement breeds more optimism and fun. Sports stars and entertainers have a powerful Sun and 5th house.

## Stage Performance

There is an innate need to be self-expressive which can express itself through drama, theater and dance. This is more about live stage performances, and the sign Leo is the most dramatic. The art of performance is a way of life.

## Love

The heart energy is of love. Love is the power that heals and gives. The Sun rules the heart and Leo is the most loyal and warm-hearted sign.

## Sun as Ruler of the 5th House

The Sun rules Leo the 5th sign of the zodiac. The Sun is what gives us light and energy and the warmth needed for life on planet earth. It is the male dominant force that projects energy. All the planets revolve around the Sun making it the center of our galaxy or solar system. It is the giver of life. The Sun is called the Atman, which reveals our spirit and life force. The Sun, Leo and the 5th house will reveal our sense of life force and energy in life.

## Leadership and Advisors

The 5th house is the house of leadership and advisors because the Sun is the powerful source of light energy and power. It gives the lead or sense of power, when flowers grow, particularly a sunflower, the flower itself turns in the direction of the sun and follows its path in the sky. Wherever the light goes we follow. Those who have the wisdom have power and leadership through a mighty 5th house.

## House of Astrology

This is the house of astrology because it is the house of advisors, for the astrologers were the advisors to the kings in ancient times. Also this is the house of creative inspiration and intelligence and to understand the science of all sciences takes a deep understanding and intelligence of life to understand astrology. It involves inspiration and insight. Astrology is mythology, psychology, mathematics, geometry, physics, and astronomy.

## Creativity

To create is to be inspired to project something outside of ourselves that outlives us. This is the 5th house. This can take place in the form of art, writing, children or inventions.

The fire that fuels the outward expression creates our extension of ourselves in the form of dating and courtship. This is the house of love and love interests, opening the heart. It is the excitement of love and love interests, but the 7th house is the house of commitments, and contracts, which have to do with agreements. But the 5th house is the house of falling in love. This is actually the house to be viewed when first meeting and finding a love interest.

## Intelligence and the Mind

This is the house of intelligence and the mind. This house gives the ability to understand concepts and ideas that are behind the creative principal. The 4th house controls the receptive energy of the mind but the 5th house is the natural intelligence that comes from previous lifetimes. Natural intelligence is what we call street smarts or common sense. Mars in this house gives deep intelligence since Mars is the planet of intelligence. Mars in the 5th house give the ability to be an engineer. They understand how things work and mechanics.

## Speculation Games and Lotteries

Benefic planets in the 5th house give benefits through speculation, games, lotteries and the stock market. When one has a clear mind, is positive then they make better choices in terms of speculation.

## Poorva-punya

Poorva-punya is good past life credit from previous lifetimes. This may be because the 5th house is the 9th house from the 9th house meaning the house of luck and fortune. But to have gifts such as talent is definitely good past life credit. People with talent are considered lucky. Talent is an innate gift from other lifetimes. Musical talent, artistic talent as in drawing, painting, sculpting, writing, drama, dance, and sports is viewed as something extraordinary and special. As small children certain aptitudes and abilities are prevalent early. This is good past life credit. Further development of these gifts leads to many successes in life.

## Vision and Seeing the Future

When in the creative zone, there is a sense of timelessness, to escape the confines of time. This is an out of body experience and the reason why this is the house of vision and ability to see the future. You escape the limits of time and the material plane through the mind.

## Crown Chakra

The crown chakra is the Sun. This may be why the crown area is what glows in halos. This is where we escape the physical world into timelessness and where we have clear vision and connection to the Divine.

In Christian faith the act of the sign of the cross the hand touches the crown chakra and then the heart. This is symbolic to connect the crown to the heart, The brain and the heart work together to give consciousness and life.

## Hair

Not to mention just how important our crowning glory is, our hair. A good hair day always makes us feel better and is a billion dollar business. The sign Leo is known to have beautiful hair as in a lion's mane.

# Bhavat Bhavam

## The Fifth House

It is the 5th from the 1st.

It is the 1st from the 5th. The basic core meaning of the 5th house is the **creative mind**. It is our mind that enables us to grow consciously, rationalize and make sense of this life. It is true intelligence, exhibiting true common sense. It relates to things we manifest or create. These creations are externalized through ourselves and lives beyond ourselves. This includes children or art. This is the house of leadership, as being an advisor or in politics. It also rules our spiritual practices. It is the house of astrologers, for they are intelligent advisors.

It is the 3rd from the 3rd house. This indicates communication skills such as writing as well as the creative arts. It is many short travels, learning and education.

It is the 9th from the 9th house. This is the father's father therefore; our grandfather as well as our father's spiritual beliefs. It is our spiritual beliefs and teachers, our spiritual pilgrimages involving foreign travel. It is the house of teachers especially of truth.

It is the 12th from the 6th house. It is the end of illness, and struggles, possibly dealing with end of debt, and the end of work as in retirement.

**It is the 6th from the 12th house.** This is work with charities or institutions, as well as work with foreigners. The work we did in a past life. It is trouble with sleep and possible bad dreams.

**It is the 11th from the 7th house.** This house is the friends of our spouse. It is our spouse's goals and aspirations as well as the attainment of these.

**It is the 7th from the 11th house.** This is our friend's spouses also indicating their goals. It is partnerships with our friends even business dealings with them.

**It is the 10th from the 8th house.** This is a career in metaphysics such as astrology, psychics or mediums, professions based on death, research, taxes or legacies.

**It is the 8th from the 10th house.** It is research done for our career or the ability to trouble shoot problems as a career or businesses. It may indicate change or end of the career.

**It is the 4th from the 2nd house.** This is real estate from the family or security from money and family.

**It is the 2nd from the 4th house.** This is the house of wealth and money from the mother, also wealth from real estate. It can indicate the mother's speech.

# Planets in the 5th House

## Sun

Sun in the 5th house gives a bright mind and clear perception and a good sense of self and confidence. There is a deep need to express through the creative force, and indicates a special gift or talent. It may limit children and usually gives male children or the 1st born will be a son. Children are powerful and strong and will make an important mark in the world. They will be advisors in their chosen fields.

## Moon

There is a gift or specific talent that will be a major focus in life. Love of knowledge and true intelligence as in common sense makes life decisions easy. Teaching and advising others comes easy. Children are an important part of life. The first-born may be a girl or there may only be one child. Spirituality is a driving force throughout life.

## Mercury

Mercury in the 5th house gives clear perception, vision and intelligence. There is a special way of communication with the need to express information and teach others. They are gifted writers and storytellers. Their great skills in speculation give an ability to guide and advise others.

## Venus

Venus in the 5th house gives wealth and profound creative talents. Benefits come through love and children. The expression of openhearted love fuels a need to find a partner and love in life. Can be good with politics for it is about finding balance and peace in the world. They have beautiful and talented children.

## Mars

Mars in the 5th house gives profound intelligence. It is the ability to understand concepts and ideas behind a philosophy. Mars gives the ability to build and create things such as in mechanics and engineers. Mathematics comes naturally especially when the sign Gemini is involved. Can cause problems with children.

## Jupiter

Jupiter in the 5th house can indicate too much energy in this house, for Jupiter is the karaka of the children and when the karaka is in the house of children this can cause problems with children. There is a very expansive and open-minded approach to life always holding on to the positive view. Positive thinking will bring positive results. A bright mind with keen intelligence brings gifts from this placement.

## Saturn

Saturn in the 5th house is a very complex placement. This can denote a very profound understanding and intelligence. Saturn indicates very serious thinking and contemplation. The thinking process takes time and appears slow but is retained with deep comprehension. This can indicate wisdom meaning great knowledge from previous lifetimes, appears as an old soul. Children can be delayed or limited but very wise and intelligent.

## Rahu

Rahu in the 5th house gives deep mental powers and ability to control many aspects and people in life. Can be a powerful advisor through deep intelligence. There is an attraction to material gains through unusual talents. Can acquire wealth and fortune, but trouble in having or raising children. A compulsive and obsessive mind keeps them in constant anxiety and mental worries.

## Ketu

Ketu in the 5th house gives a deep connection to the Divine and intensely spiritual view of the world. There is a profound understanding and compassion. The mind is plagued by obsessive ideas and will have the tendency to be consumed with conspiracy and paranoid ideas. Children may be a major worry and concern. Overprotective tactics can be overwhelming, for there is an innate fear of harm to their children and they feel they can never do enough for them.

# Ruler of the 5th House in the

## 5th House

A powerful strong intelligence directs the life with clear intentions and focus. Creativity gives a specific interest in the arts or self-expression. They are advisors in their fields of expertise. Children are an important part o their life.

## 6th House

There may be a struggle to have children. Talents are put to practical use to achieve their goals. Many gains come from children. Hard work will pay off and bring success in life.

## 7th House

Children will play an important role in relationships or marriage. Children may work with the spouse. The partner is talented and successful in life with many friends and associations.

## 8th House

Problems around having children can be a major issue in life. Children may go through difficulty due conflict and possible divorce. There is a powerful intelligence that is directed in research producing new discoveries.

## 9<sup>th</sup> House

Spirituality and philosophical studies are a dominant part of life involving teaching and writing spiritual truths. The paternal grandfather can be a major influence in life. There is an ease and comfort that comes from a certain amount of luck.

## 10<sup>th</sup> House

Teaching is a possible profession particularly with children. This is a powerful position for those who are sought out as advisors in their field. They can be successful in careers in speculation such as the stock market.

## 11<sup>th</sup> House

Strong connections to friends and associates lead to powerful connections that put them in positions of influence and power in the community. There can be a strong interest in politics. They are well liked and have many friends.

## 12<sup>th</sup> House

There are issues and problems around children or they may not be able to have them. Children may be taken away as in divorce or moving away from home once grown. Interest in films or movies can be a positive expression of their gifts.

## 1<sup>st</sup> House

There is a specific talent and gift to be developed in this lifetime. Luck and ease seems to come their way. Intelligence and mental focus gives them authority and prominence in life. Children bring blessings.

## 2<sup>nd</sup> House

Financial status comes from a clear intelligent mind that can contemplate and think things through. Money is gained from speculation and analysis. Children bring financial opportunities in life.

## 3<sup>rd</sup> House

Creativity is a major component in life, for the need to express is very strong. There is a drive to communicate and pass on valuable information, which may inspire them to write a book.

## 4<sup>th</sup> House

Home life and domestic skills can be a major part of their life. Children remain close to home and support the family. The mother is very close and takes on an important role in the children's lives.

**Steven Spielberg** is an iconic movie producer and director. Winner of the academy award for best picture, Schindler's List and an Oscar for Saving Private Ryan. His lists of movies entail many of those that shape a generation. He is pure genius with incredible talent. Growing up he felt like an outcast due to his parents constantly moving and being the only Jewish kid in the class. It is no wonder he immersed himself into his creative ability, working with film at an early age.

| 10th h. | 11th h. | 12th h. | 1st h. |
|---|---|---|---|
| ♓ | ♈ | ♉ ☊ 18:37 Roh / ♅℞ 26:22 Mrg | ♊ ASC 17:40 Ard |
| 9th h. ♒ | Steven Spielberg | | 2nd h. ♋ ♄℞ 15:02 Pus / ♆℞ 19:59 Asl |
| 8th h. ♑ | Wed 12-18-1946 18:16:00 Cincinnati, OH, Ohio USA Timezone: 5 DST: 0 Latitude: 39N09'00 Longitude: 84W27'00 Ayanamsha : -23:06:42 Lahiri | | 3rd h. ♌ |
| 7th h. ♐ ♂ 08:01 Mul / ☉ 03:20 Mul | 6th h. ♏ ☿ 14:41 Anu / ☋ 18:37 Jye | 5th h. ♎ ☽ 13:44 Swa / ♃ 24:49 Vis / ♀ 26:08 Vis | 4th h. ♍ ♇ 17:31 Has |

*Chart 3: Steven Spielberg*

The 5<sup>th</sup> house is the house of talent, creative ability and in terms of money it is the house of speculation and intelligence. In this most wonderful house Spielberg has the 2 natural money planets both Venus and Jupiter. The signs that Venus is the most powerful for wealth are Taurus, Libra and Pisces in which has been a common denominator in many wealth-producing charts of the mega rich. He has Venus in Libra, which is in the house of talent and intelligence (5<sup>th</sup> house) which Venus also has ruler ship over this blessed house. Additionally, Venus is magnified by the aspect of the conjunction of Jupiter in this house. Next to both Jupiter and Venus is the Moon, which rules the 2<sup>nd</sup> house of money. The 5<sup>th</sup> house ruler with the 2<sup>nd</sup> house ruler in the powerful 5<sup>th</sup> house both conjunct Jupiter expanding their power all the more. The planets in the 5<sup>th</sup> house Jupiter, Venus and the Moon also aspects the 11<sup>th</sup> house by opposition. Any planets in the 5<sup>th</sup> house always aspect the 11<sup>th</sup> house, which is powerful for wealth and great gains. The Moon ruler of the 2<sup>nd</sup> house is conjunct both natural benefics for wealth in the 5<sup>th</sup> house of creativity and aspects the 11<sup>th</sup> house of gains.

*Henry Rousseau* was a French Post Impressionist painter. He was ridiculed during his lifetime but came to be known as self-taught genius. Critics judged his paintings of jungles to be childish but finally became esteemed works of art for they realized his sophistication with specific techniques. Pablo Picasso revered Rousseau and today his works are considered artistic masterpieces.

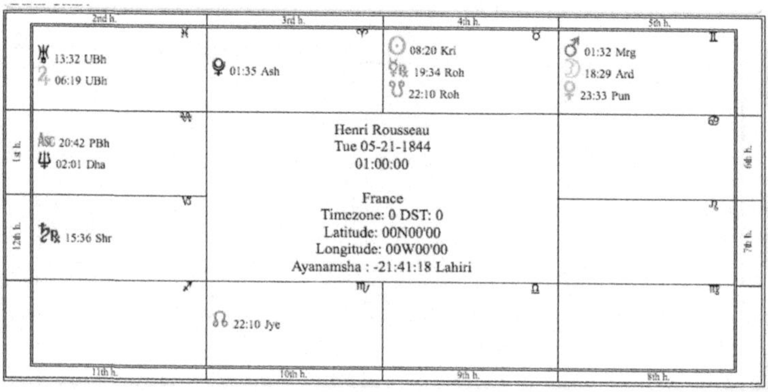

*Chart 4: Henry Rousseau*

In Rousseau's 5th house he has Mars, Moon, and Venus in Gemini.

Mars in the 5th house gives great passion and intelligence but in the sign Gemini it is very adaptable and indicates his ingenious sophisticated artistic techniques. Mars rules the 3rd house of creativity with his hands and the 10th house of his career as an artist. The Moon gives his great sensitivity in his work through feeling and color, but as ruler of the 6th house of obstacles he was ridiculed and claimed his art was childish. Venus in the 5th is his mark of a great artist as it is the most powerful planet for creativity and the arts. Venus rules the 9th house of luck and fortune and the 4th house of power and happiness. Actually, the 4th house can be a house of royalty and fame.

# The 9$^{th}$ House: Truth and Judgment

*All I have seen teaches me to trust the creator for all I have not see.*

*Ralph Waldo Emerson 1803-1882*

*Would you rather be right or would you rather be happy?*

*A Course in Miracles*

**Bhagya Bhava.** Spirituality, beliefs, gurus, father, fortune, luck, long travels, pilgrimages or journeys to gain spiritual knowledge, teaching, teachers, colleges of higher learning, publications, law and lawyers, hips and thighs.

**Trikona, Dharma.**

## Spirituality

The 9$^{th}$ house is the house of spiritual teaching. It is the house of high-minded teaching that defines who we are in a spiritual reference. Spirituality is our being that is deep beneath our physical reality, it is the essence that transcends the body.

This house is teaching that concerns the spiritual energy which when felt fills us with inspiration and we feel the need to extend this information to all who can benefit from this knowledge. This is the extension of spiritual knowledge to others in the form of spiritual teachings.

## Religious Teachings

The spiritual information acquired through the $9^{th}$ house can come from religious teachings that inspire us to have moments of revelation, but it is usually acquired through the spoken and written words of those who have passed on this information. These inspirations are from teachers, priests, or gurus of present or ancient times.

It does require the belief, trust and faith that these teachings are the way to the truth. So the $9^{th}$ house is the house of trust and faith. It gives comfort that a teacher or guide can direct and shine light on our path.

## Devotion

The way provided by these spiritual gurus does require blind faith, which can be defined as devotion. And when someone devotes their life to a cause they believe in they can become blissful with the connection to their belief. It takes away all the worries of finding their way in mass confusion and simplifies their connection to the Divine. They have the way devised for them and all they have to do is follow the simple rules of their path.

Unfortunately, many can become obsessed that their way is the only way, and feel they must convince others to believe their way as the only way to obtain spirituality. Because it involves blind faith the means to enforce their beliefs onto others becomes irrational. They tend to demonize the ways of others in order to glorify their way.

This behavior seems to bring separation and alienation to others as many religious institutions separate instead of uniting humanity. The power in believing one belief is more superior than the other can have a negative effect on humanity. This becomes a powerful force of separation through righteousness and condemnation. This can be an aspect of religious teachings to control with fear. This creates the negative side of religious teachings instilling guilt and shame onto others who aren't following the path of the most pious revered teachings of truth.

But what exactly is the truth? Is there only one way or one truth? Most believe in one truth. And when people believe in only one way many life situations produce hypocritical experiences that don't measure up to the expectations the teachings promise.

## Beliefs

This is because individualized beliefs get mixed into the picture of their religious teachings and begin to muddy the waters of the spiritual essence. It is extremely difficult, if not impossible to keep the spiritual essence free from individualized beliefs. Beliefs are the way that we view our world through the lens of our perception. We all have a different perspective, which is based on our worldly experiences. This comes from our birth, culture, family, birth order, heritage, parents, school, friends and any other view we may have experienced, and even previous lifetimes. So everyone's sense of truth may be a bit different and this is based on our beliefs.

## Law of Nature

The law of nature is the law of truth, which is never hypocritical and is always consistent. The law of nature is also the law of science, meaning the law of cause and effect. These laws do not have exceptions, as many humans tend to insert into their teachings in order to allow their wants and desires to be granted through their teachings. This is how many tend to justify their behaviors to get what they want, but if it is not in the natural laws of nature it will not bring enlightenment. It only confuse and divert them from the truth. This is a part of many religions that convolute the truth to manipulate teachings to control the masses.

Because the 9th house is a house of spirit, the force of this house can be very enticing as the evangelist priest's enthusiasm captivates the masses of followers that will not think for themselves. Children are lead to believe the teachings handed down. They are so impressionable with no powers of discernment, and are not to question the teachings of their parents or teachers.

This is how many belief systems are instilled at a very early age. It is very hard to break these patterns. Their life experiences are based on this philosophy and have given them the results of what they believe. Such as some of the stereotypes that we are lead to believe. Some stereotypes can be unconscious beliefs and can direct our behavior in many ways. This all comes from our beliefs acquired in early childhood.

When we are filled with the overpowering need to extend this information we may tend to confuse it with our beliefs.

## Free Will

The most powerful revelation that is so freeing of the 9th house is the fact that we have the power of choice or free will. This gives us the ability to actually choose what we believe if we can release the power of our past beliefs. This is why this is the house of luck and fortune because we can become our own masters in the ability to actually choose our fate through free will. The realization of this fact can free our soul; this comes from freeing our minds from the beliefs that confine us.

## Teachers and Gurus

As the 9th house is the house of teachers, gurus, and the father it relates to those who give guidance in life. Our father is the one who is the head of the family and provides guidance for the family, particularly the children. The guru is thought to be a spiritual teacher that is all knowing and can provide wisdom to understand life and how to make important decisions. The guru and father are known to provide important guidance in life.

## College and Higher Learning

The 9th house is the house of college and higher learning, teachers or professors associated with this academic process. This house determines the experience and opportunities of college. It can indicate any form of higher learning that is beyond high school.

The 3rd house as the opposing house is about undergraduate schooling, grade school to high school as the 9th house is higher learning as in college.

## Long Distance Travel

The 9th and 3rd house are both about travel, but the 3rd house is short distant travels and the 9th house concerns long distant travels. Sometimes travels concern spiritual pilgrimages, for the 9th house confers a sense of learning and expansion of our awareness through travel. Travel can teach and open our minds to another perspective on life.

Travel for spiritual knowledge as in spiritual pilgrimages can take us to a place that connects us on a deep soul level to places that represent our truth and feelings to a place of our spiritual roots. Many travel to India to understand the teachings of yoga, Ayurveda, and Vedic astrology. Or Christians may feel a need to travel to the holy land where Jesus, Christ was born and lived in Israel. To study art or science in the places of the original place where it began becomes inspirational in the learning process such as arts in Europe or acupuncture in China.

## Law and Justice

As the 9th house pertains to truth it also indicates the law whether it is spiritual truth, which pertains to the law of nature or man made laws to contain order and peace on the planet. So the 9th house is about the legal process and the laws of the land such as government laws, lawyers and judges. A powerful 9th house can indicate someone who goes into law as a profession. It is the house of justice and judgment. Any laws that organize governments and keep regulations are a part of the 9th house process so it concerns immigration and naturalization of a country.

The 9th house concerns legal representation such as the lawyer in a court case but the 6th house is the house of legal battles since it is the house of enemies and struggles.

## Publishing

In terms of communications and writings the 9th house is about publically displaying written materials worldwide, therefore is the house of publications. Publishing books and spreading information to the masses is an important way to distribute a message.

This is the house of luck and fortune for it is an opening to information that gives freedom. To travel worldwide is to give a sense of freedom and higher education which gives freedom to the mind for it eliminates ignorance. The ultimate freedom is from limited beliefs; a sense of adventure and a positive frame of mind will bring fortune and luck. As the 5th from the 5th house the 9th house magnifies the ability for luck. Jupiter is the planet of luck (natural ruler of Sagittarius, the ninth sign) and can be associated with the grace of God, meaning the miracles of forgiveness.

## Grandchildren

As the 5th from the 5th house it indicates the joys of grandchildren, our children's children. Jupiter ruler of the 9th sign Sagittarius is the karaka for children.

## Philosophical Studies

The sign Sagittarius is a powerful sign for force and direction as the archer points his arrow at the desired target. It is a sign for philosophical studies and thought. It is the house of philosophy, probing ideas as to the essence of reality. But it can also be a place of opinions, views and philosophies of life. This again is a thought process based on the opinions and beliefs of an individual. In reality God or nature doesn't have opinions.

## Rules the Hips

The hips are the part of the body that are ruled by the 9<sup>th</sup> house which give direction to our movement and connects our torso to the legs which give us the ability to move forward in life. The body is connected to the ground and earth through the legs, which is powered through the hips. Elderly people seem to fall and break their hips, which generally takes away their freedom to move and this destroys the desire to live. Our hips are the gateway to life and freedom.

## Bhavat Bhavam

### The Ninth House

It is the 9<sup>th</sup> from the 1<sup>st</sup> .

It is the 1<sup>st</sup> from the 9<sup>th</sup>. The 9<sup>th</sup> house's core meaning is our **beliefs.** One of the main things misunderstood in this world is the power of our beliefs. The 9<sup>th</sup> house is the house of our spirituality and this is based on our belief system. They say if you can change the way you think, you can change your life. Your thinking is based on your beliefs about yourself and your world. With strong faith and positive beliefs you can create a more fortunate life. This is the house of fortune. It also represents our teachers as in higher education, father, and gurus. It is the house of the truth. Our quest for the truth will form our beliefs, which in essence is our quest for God consciousness. Since this is the house of truth it becomes the house of the law and lawyers. The ultimate truth is the spiritual truth that is governed by karma. This house rules righteousness and judgment thus, can cause separation instead of union, which is more a 12<sup>th</sup> house feature. It is long distance travel particularly spiritual pilgrimages. We need to watch that our judgments do not turn into resentments that could separate ourselves from truth. The need to be right must not outweigh our need to be compassionate and loving. This is the house for the third born child.

It is the 5<sup>th</sup> from the 5<sup>th</sup> house. This is our children's children therefore; it is our grandchildren. It can particularly pertain to our first born children. It is advice and spiritual council received and given. It is the creative mind and wisdom.

It is the 11<sup>th</sup> from the 11<sup>th</sup> house. This is the house of our ultimate desires, the achievement of these goals, desires, great gains and luck. This house will indicate how well you are liked.

**It is the 2nd from the 8th house.** This can be money made from other people such as winnings or the money received from inheritances.

**It is the 8th from the 2nd house.** This house can indicate money received from other people such as in inheritances or from death.

**It is the 3rd from the 7th house.** This reveals the communication and travels we have with the spouse. It is the spouse's siblings (brother or sister in law).

**It is the 7th from the 3rd house.** This house indicates our sibling's spouse, particularly the youngest. It can indicate a business partnership with siblings.

**It is the 4th from the 6th house.** It is happiness and security from work, or our efforts.

**It is the 6th from the 4th house.** This is the house of the health of the mother. It can indicate work that is done out of the home.

**It is the 10th from the 12th house.** This can be a career from foreign trade or a vocation with charities.

**It is the 12th from the 10th house.** This house can indicate retirement because it is the end to the career.

## Planets in the 9th House

### Sun

Interest in travel and higher education such as college and University are a focus. The Sun as a malefic and overpowering can indicate problems with the father who can be very overbearing and controlling. Teachers can be ego centered and demanding. Spirituality and philosophy is an area that can consume the attention for good and bad. An overzealous and fanatical attitude can dominate the behavior. Law can be a direction in higher studies. A legal profession is indicated with planets in the 9th house. The first-born grandchild will be a boy. A brother in law can cause problems for the family

## Moon

Unpredictable behavior of the father causes concern and problems in family matters. The first grandchild may be a girl. Travel and world affairs direct a life calling. Travel is a passion; world travels open the mind and awareness. Uncertainty in beliefs vacillates in philosophical and religious views. Women teachers cause confusion or can change your life course and direction. A sister in law stirs up problems in the family.

## Mercury

Travel and education are the focus throughout life. An academic life style is well suited. Teaching and giving direction comes easy, and may indicate life as a professor. Intelligence and open mindedness in philosophical and spiritual subjects may indicate a career in inspiring others to a new way of thinking and believing. The father is very intelligent and could be a teacher. The spouse is well traveled. Publishing and mass communications can be a part of the career. Literary skills are indicated

## Venus

Blessings and wealth can come from the father. Understanding and compassion are a means of communication, reflecting great social skills. Grandchildren bring fulfillment and love to the family. Strong spiritual beliefs give comfort and gratification as a trust in faith directs life. In a males chart the wife is spiritual and educated with a love of travel. A sister in law brings peace and happiness to the family.

## Mars

The desire to argue and be righteous can lead to a career in the legal profession. The father may be of the military, police, fireman or an athlete. He can be pushy and demanding, causing unrest and difficulty for the family. A strong urge to push opinions on others can drive people away. A drive to travel can orient the life's calling, as in working for an airline. The spouse's brother will cause big problems and should be avoided in any family business.

## Jupiter

Spirituality is a focus throughout life and an urge to teach and inspire others dominates the life's purpose. A teacher of morality and truth compels and gives life meaning and purpose. Philosophical studies are the driving force of the consciousness. World travel opens the mind and heart. The father can benefit the individual in many ways particularly financially, but may be too extreme. There will be many grandchildren. Benefits come from the partner's siblings. This is a placement of luck and fortune.

## Saturn

The father may be stern and controlling with many rules and regulations. The spiritual beliefs may be traditional and structured or from ancient origins. Opportunities for travel seem to limit the individual in the scope of culture and new perspectives. College is difficult and teachers are hard on the individual. There may be no grandchildren or distance and limitation to seeing them. The spouse may be an only child or is not connected to their siblings.

## Rahu

The father can be very stern, out of control, with an addictive personality. Fanatical views on the world in terms of politics and religion cloud the mind. Travel is impulsive and spontaneous. Problems around travel may bring troubles and loss. There is an attraction to extremist teachers that have a controlling edge like a cult leader. There is an attraction to cults and far out beliefs. The spouse should not go into business with a sibling, for there is the possibility of a split in the family from corruption or extreme differences in opinion. A split or miscommunication with grandchildren may drive them away or they may live far away.

## Ketu

Spirituality is a burning desire and focus throughout the life. Many of life's circumstances lead one to want enlightenment of the soul. The father is not present, physically, mentally or emotionally. But there is a deep desire to connect with him for there seems to be a void or emptiness concerning the father. The eternal quest is in finding the truth in all matters. A career in teaching religion, or spirituality is possible. Travel to unusual places such as a spiritual pilgrimage brings a feeling of connection. Grandchildren may have emotional or physical problems. There is disconnection with the spouse's in-laws.

# Ruler of the 9<sup>th</sup> house in the

## 9<sup>th</sup> House

Philosophy and spirituality are an eternal quest. Teaching and traveling are a way of life. The father has a major impact or influence on the life.

## 10<sup>th</sup> House

The father inspires or initiates the career or profession. There are fortunate circumstances and great opportunities involved with the career and reputation. This is a very lucky position and gives a great career.

## 11<sup>th</sup> House

Connections and blessings come through friends and groups or organizations. Spiritual groups bring fulfillment and happiness. The father has great connections and will be a friend throughout life.

## 12<sup>th</sup> House

A deep spiritual quest initiates travel to many places, some may be foreign. The ability to forgive and live a life of spiritual commitment brings enlightenment. Profound spiritual experiences enrich the life.

## 1<sup>st</sup> House

A spiritual conscientious attitude is reflected throughout life. Truthfulness is a definite virtue. A search for meaning and purpose is sought through a life of living in balance in accordance to beliefs.

## 2<sup>nd</sup> House

Speech is clear, direct and truthful with a complete aversion to others who are untruthful. They may be speakers or lecturers. Wealth and fortune comes at various times and could come from the father.

## 3<sup>rd</sup> House

World travel and learning are a major part of life. The siblings can be a great benefit throughout life. Spirituality is a lifelong study. Writing skills are indicated.

## 4<sup>th</sup> House

The mother may be very spiritual, making sure religious studies are pursued. There is a desire for a beautiful home in faraway places. The father and mother are close and stay together.

## 5<sup>th</sup> House

The father is a great teacher and is very close to the individual. Spiritual teachings are a passion and could be a profession. Luck and fortune comes from investments and children.

## 6<sup>th</sup> House

The legal profession may be sought out as a career or the individual may need the use of lawyers at specific times. The father may struggle or have health problems.

## 7<sup>th</sup> House

A spiritual partner can bring many blessings to life. If female they are attracted to a partner that reminds them of their father.

## 8<sup>th</sup> House

The father has a life of torment, problems and secrets usually inflicting the children, or he could die early. There is an interest in metaphysical studies or distaste for religions.

*Deepak Chopra* started out as a medical doctor but ended up as a famous metaphysical teacher with many published books and speaking engagements worldwide. His ascendant is Aquarius, which is ruled by Saturn. His Saturn resides in his 6th house of healing and service. He was initially drawn to the healing profession, as he became a medical doctor.

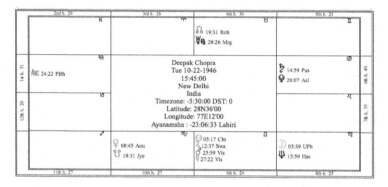

*Chart 5: Deepak Chopra*

The 9th house stands out where four major planets reside. The 9th house rules philosophy, spirituality, teaching, and publishing. All the indicators of the 10 house of career are in the 9th house, Sun, Jupiter and Mars. The ruler of the 9th house is in the 10th house further indicating a 9th house career. When there is a connection of the 9th and the 10 houses this will bring luck and fortune to the individual, concerning their career and social standing. He has the ruler of the 9th house, Venus in the 10th house in Scorpio, which is ruled by Mars in the 9th house. They both exchanges signs with Mars in Libra the sign Venus rules and Venus in Scorpio the sign Mars rules. The connection of the 9th and 10th houses can produce fame. Deepak is a public speaker on spirituality and publishes many books.

He is a speaker and a writer of international acclaim. The 2nd house ruler Jupiter is how he makes his money. The 2nd house ruler in the 9th house means he makes his money in publishing and speaking on subjects of spirituality and philosophy. Mars as ruler of the 10th house of career also rules his 3rd house of writing. His acclaim is through his many published books on spirituality and healing.

The Moon in his 8th house and ruler of the 6th house of health and healing can represent his deep quest to uncover the truth in healing and can represent a doctor who does surgery.

Jupiter ruler of both the 2nd house and 11th house is his great money-producing planet. Jupiter is in the 9th house of luck, and opportunities. Jupiter in the 9th house aspects the 1st and the 5th houses, which empowers his creativity for writing plus, Mercury ruler of the 5th house is with Jupiter ruler of the money houses. This all adds up to wealth, money, and opportunities to speak and inspire others to explore his teachings of spiritual truth.

*Pope Francis* (Jorge Mario Bergoglio) began his Papacy March 13, 2013. He came after the resignation of Pope Benedict XVI. Throughout his life both as an individual and spiritual leader Bergoglio was noted for his humility. His main concern has always been for the poor and believes in building bridges between people of all backgrounds, beliefs, and faiths.

| 12th h. 22 | | 1st h. 29 | | 2nd h. 30 | | 3rd h. 31 |
|---|---|---|---|---|---|---|
| | ♅℞ 12:56 Ash<br>Asc 26:51 Kri | | | ☊ 01:17 Mrg | | |
| ♄ 23:30 PBh | Pope Francis<br>Thu 12-17-1936<br>17:10:00<br>Buenos Aires, Distrito Federal<br>Argentina | | ♀℞ 05:18 Pus | | | |
| ☽ 17:29 Shr<br>♀ 14:26 Shr | Timezone: 4 DST: 1<br>Latitude: 34S35'00<br>Longitude: 58W40'00<br>Ayanamsha : -22:58:53 Lahiri | | ♆ 25:58 PPh | | | |
| ☿ 18:35 PSh<br>♃ 10:31 Mul<br>☉ 02:45 Mul<br>☋ 01:17 Mul | | | ♂ 26:26 Cht | | | |
| 9th h. 24 | | 8th h. 31 | | 7th h. 3? | | 6th h. 34 |

*Chart 6: Pope Francis*

Pope Francis has a beautiful 9th house with planets Mercury, Jupiter, Sun and Rahu. The 9th house as the house of spiritual teachings fits well with a pope's life of teaching the religious truth that he believes in. In the sign of Sagittarius he is a believer in finding the truth and travels far and wide to spread his philosophy. The Sun is inspiration and rules the 5th house as he inspires others to seek the truth. Jupiter is the ruler of the 9th house in the 9th house indicating a life of teaching and strong beliefs, but as Jupiter also rules the 12th house he surrendered his life to his spirituality.

Mercury the planet of learning and education rules the 3rd house of teaching and communications, and the 6th house of service indicates his life as a teacher who gives his life to serve. Powerful Rahu magnifies all of this energy. With his 9th house Pope Francis is following his dharma and destiny and he will be a magnificent Pope because he believes wholeheartedly in his work and his mission in life as a spiritual teacher.

# Part II

## The Earth Triplicity - Artha Houses

### 2<sup>nd</sup> House, 6<sup>th</sup> House, and 10<sup>th</sup> House

*"I am not what happened to me, I am what I choose to become.*

*Carl G. Jung*

### Artha

The artha houses are 2, 6 and 10. They relate to the three earth signs (earth triplicity). The 2<sup>nd</sup> house relates to the first earth sign Taurus, the sixth Virgo, and the tenth Capricorn. These houses define our material achievements, and the recognition gained from them. The 2<sup>nd</sup> house is about wealth and the material possessions gained. The 6<sup>th</sup> house is the urge to improve through hard work. The 10<sup>th</sup> house is the public recognition received through a career.

The earth triangle is about our material achievements, and the recognition gained from them. Houses 2, 6, and 10 relate to the three earth signs Taurus, Virgo, and Capricorn.

The 2<sup>nd</sup> house and sign Taurus is about the material possessions gained, and the money we earn. These are the comforts of life, and are sometimes a symbol of our success in life.

The 6<sup>th</sup> house and sign Virgo is a house of work. It also symbolizes the things we will do to improve ourselves. It governs the actions necessary to achieve our goals. It is the daily grind within the workplace.

The 10th house and sign Capricorn is our desire for recognition through our work. This is the career house. We typically spend more than half our life focused upon realizing these goals of wealth, and recognition for all our work and achievements.

The houses and signs of the earth triangle work together to achieve our goals of material wealth through self-effort and work.

These are the areas of:

- achievement, possessions, and wealth (2nd house),
- the urge to improve oneself through hard work (6th house), and
- the public recognition received through a career (10th house).

These are the artha houses – the houses of material wealth and of recognition for our achievements.

The earth element is our physical body, or the material world. It rules over our material comforts and gives us earthly pleasures. Taurus is the first earth sign; five signs away is the next earth sign, Virgo, and nine signs from Taurus is the third earth sign, Capricorn. This is called the earth triplicity. Taurus is the second sign in the natural zodiac, Virgo the sixth, and Capricorn the tenth. Houses 2, 6 and 10 are the houses of our material, physical world, and our pursuits to gain recognition. These are called the artha houses.

# The 2ⁿᵈ House: Self Worth and Wealth

*I have about concluded that wealth is a state of mind, and that anyone can acquire a wealthy state of mind by thinking rich thoughts.*

*Andrew Young*

**Dhana Bhava:** Early childhood, domestic life, food or substances ingested, drinking habits, education, wealth, money, voice, speech, face, teeth, neck, vision in general, right eye in particular.

**Maraka. Artha.**

## Early Childhood

The 2ⁿᵈ house pertains to our early childhood following our birth. This involves all areas of family experience in life. It is the house of family happiness, which actually conditions the ability to have a happy family environment. Because early childhood and family environment takes in a vast array of life's experiences this house can combine many aspects of human life and existence.

## Money and Finances

This is an Artha house meaning it pertains to our ability to find protection and security from the world or earthly experiences. This is the house that pertains to money and finances since this is a huge part of our earthly experiences in terms of life comforts, and is also about our sense of self worth.

Our sense of self worth or achievement comes through our ability to make money and thrive in the material world. This is the house of finances and money and our ability to make money. This concerns the constant influx of money, paycheck or income to care for our families.

This is relative to the 2nd sign, Taurus. Taurus is a fixed earth sign know to be reliable and constant, so this house deals with income that comes in the way of a paycheck from our businesses.

The Artha houses pertain to our way of making a living in providing income to buy the things we need to live our lives in the earthly plane. These are essentials to physical life.

## What Goes into and Comes out of the Mouth

Interestingly, it rules the mouth, which gives us the ability to take in the food we need to nourish the physical body. The 6th house is about the digestion of foods. The 6th house and Virgo pertain to our health and our daily activities that give health.

## Work and Income

Artha houses pertain to our work in terms of making money. The 2nd house is our income, the 6th house is our working conditions and daily matters, and the 10th house is our career and the pursuit of happiness through our work.

## Addictions

This is the house that pertains to what we consume through our mouth and can determine if we eat healthy or unhealthy foods. It indicates if someone consumes toxins and poisons such as drugs and alcohol. This house may determine addictions if there are malefic planets. Malefic planets transiting through this house can indicate taking in addictive substances or poisonous foods and can indicate food poisoning.

## Voice

As the 2nd house deals with the mouth it also pertains to our voice and the ability to express through the voice. Communication skills are a part of the 3rd house and the 2nd house, and overlap when pertaining to matters of speech and communications. The 2nd house is the house for the voice for singing, speaking and teaching. This is the house that gives gifts of the voice.

## The Need to be Heard

Issues of speaking and the need to be heard are interchanged with the 2nd to the 3rd houses. Actual speaking is the 2nd house but the need to be heard is the 3rd house. Speech and the voice in terms of the quality and sound of the voice is a 2nd house matter. The 2nd house rules the mouth and throat and the 3rd house rules hearing and the ears.

Someone not heard in early childhood is reflected in a person's sense of self-esteem and will be indicated throughout life. This can definitely interfere with someone's ability to make money and provide for their family, for they don't feel a good sense self-confidence because they were discounted in childhood. This corrupts their ability to be successful in terms of making money.

A powerful voice goes hand in hand with the ability to be successful in making money and feeling self- esteem. Early conditions in childhood can determine this sense of self worth and the ability to be strong and independent in material matters.

## Eye Sight

The 2nd house also rules your ability to see, as in physical eyesight and difficult planets here can cause problems with vision. This can be taken figuratively as well, for they may not have a vision or cannot see their life easily.

The Sun and the Moon (the lights of astrology) rule vision, and when in the 2nd house can harm the vision or eyesight. The transit of malefic planets here can predict when the eyesight declines.

## Teeth

Since it rules the mouth this house rules the teeth and can indicate strong teeth or dental problems depending on the planets here.

Since it is the house of early childhood and the mouth it is the house of oral fixations and can be the house that determines food addictions and weight problems, such as anorexia and bulimia.

## Face

The entire face comes under the ruler ship of the 2nd house as to an attractive or unattractive face. The face is the front we use to project ourselves to the world using our voice and vision. An attractive face can open many doors and give self-confidence.

## Self Esteem and Confidence

What can be surmised through the analysis of this house is that it essentially concerns our sense of self-esteem and self worth, whether you are looking at early childhood, money, our face, voice, family, weight problems, vision and our smile.

## Thyroid

In terms of the throat area and the neck and the 2nd sign Taurus this house concerns the thyroid gland and can indicate the way we metabolize our foods and symbolically how we metabolize the process of life. Thyroid conditions can be seen through this house or the sign Taurus. What we feel about ourselves, and our life has an effect on how we metabolize foods.

## Eating and Diet

Planets connecting the 2nd house with the 6th house have to do with eating, diet and foods.

## Domestic Happiness

Since the 2nd house has to do with family or domestic happiness it has a lot to do with marital happiness or unhappiness. This is a house that can predict divorce since it is the 8th house from the 7th house. Difficult planets here either in the natal chart or transiting can cause major problems in a marriage or business partners.

Jupiter is a karaka of the 2nd house and its placement here can give optimism and wealth.

The ruler of the 2nd house can be a decisive clue as to how someone will make money in life.

## Maraka House

The 2nd and 7th houses are the maraka houses. Maraka means "killer. This means these houses have a grave effect on the length of life. This is because the houses of length of life or longevity are the 8th and 3rd houses. It is because both the 2nd and the 7th houses are 12th from the houses of longevity. It is seen that at the time of death a person will be in a dasha of a planet ruling or in a maraka house, either 2nd or 7th houses.

# Bhavat Bhavam

## The Second House

### The 2nd from the 1st.

**The 1st from the 2nd.** The core issue of the 2nd house is based on **our values**. This is developed in early childhood with our upbringing. This is the house of material wealth we have acquired on our own. In our materialistic society our sense of value is generally based on our wealth or money. Money gives power. Early childhood and domestic happiness fall into this domain as well. Strong values give a sense of self worth and confidence. This is figuratively our vision or how we see things, as well as our physical eyesight. It is what goes into and out of our mouth pertaining to the things we ingest such as foods, drinks and speech.

**It is the 12th from the 3rd house.** It is the loss of will power, or the desire to live. This is what makes the 2nd house a maraka house. Maraka means death or killer. It is secret conquests. Death could be a secret conquest.

**It is the 3rd from the 12 house.** This is the will or courage to see our denials or shadows. It is foreign trade such as import or export, sales of foreign items and travel to foreign counties.

**It is the 11th from the 4th house.** It is wealth from fixed assets such as real estate. It is the mother's desires, friends, and achievement of security.

**It is the 4th from the 11th house.** This is security, real estate or fixed assets from the oldest sibling. The wealth acquired from our fixed assets.

**It is the 10th from the 5th house.** It is our children's career pursuits, fame or fortune. It indicates recognition for being an advisor, such as the advice of an astrologer or councilor. It is what our intelligence brings, especially for our career pursuits.

**It is the 5th from the 10th house.** This is the intelligence and advice given by our leaders or bosses. It also reveals how intelligent you are perceived, and the recognition received. It will reveal information about your boss' children.

**It is the 9th from the 6th house.** It is luck from aunts and uncles, spiritual service and how we believe we are helpful to others. It indicates blessings received from employees or pets. It may be travel for work or jobs of a service nature.

**It is the 6th from the 9ᵗʰ house**. This house indicates the work involved in spiritual pursuits and studies. It is the house for the father's health and work.

**It is the 8ᵗʰ from the 7th house**. This house indicates death of the spouse, bankruptcy or even chronic illnesses. Indications of this house are humiliation, disgrace or betrayal from the spouse. It is the house for divorce.

**It is the 7ᵗʰ from the 8ᵗʰ house**. It is partnerships based on money, corruption or power.

# Planets in the 2ⁿᵈ house

## Sun

The Sun in the 2ⁿᵈ house can burn a hole in the financial pockets of the individual. The Sun is a malefic and can cause burn out in the area it sits. There is a focus on money matters. Finances and money seem to cause many ups and downs and problems in life. There is a burning desire to find success through financial independence. Difficult experiences in early life disturb the ability to find security and peace in later years. Once the realization of the blocks from early childhood are uncovered and self-confidence is restored financial success will be granted. This may be the culprit of emotional problems that create life's obstacles. Eyesight can be stressed and this may indicate poor eyesight. The Sun here can also cause problems for teeth, especially if it is in a difficult sign, like Libra.

## Moon

Early childhood was fraught with many changes and disruptions. There was no sense of peace or security. The family was under financial stress or circumstances that caused unrest. The mother was under duress and mental turmoil. There may have been many changes in residence in early life. Financial matters fluctuate causing mental instability and problems with marriage. Sensitivity with certain foods causes problems with digestion. Denial of emotional issues may create marital problems in latter life Growth through living in the truth will heal family matters. The eyesight may be weak.

## Mercury

Education and learning are emphasized in the early years. Communication skills are developed at an early age. Speech begins early and progresses quickly. There is an aptitude for learning foreign languages, and interest in foreign cultures. Financial success and income are acquired through businesses of sales, marketing or travel. Humor is a means to entertain and captivate others. It comes in handy in convincing others to invest in their products, inventions or way of thinking.

## Venus

Depending on the sign Venus occupies wealth can be acquired. If Venus is in the signs Libra, Taurus or Pisces there is the ability to acquire massive wealth. Childhood and family life will give a sense of contentment and happiness. Financial security gives comfort and relaxation. Living the life of luxury appeals to the senses. Married life and family will be comforting with many happy reunions and family gatherings. Careful with consumption of sweets for this can indicate problems with digestion of sugars or indicate thyroid problems.

## Mars

Speech is developed early, but care and thought should be taken before blurting out any opinions. Speech can be cutting and offensive. There are problems in early childhood with much fighting and conflict usually surmounting in the parents separating or divorce. There can be torment from other siblings. Problems with sore throats are common in childhood, for what the individual has to say is not valued. Problems with self worth inflict the individual throughout life. Eating can be a problem for there never appears to be enough time to sit down and have a proper meal. Eating on the go or in a hurry can cause digestive problems. This can be a strong placement for great money and wealth, for they are driven and ambitious.

## Jupiter

Wealth and money comes easy to this individual, especially if Jupiter is in Pisces or Sagittarius. There will definitely be high times in this placement. A powerful voice can direct and dictate many opportunities in life. This can indicate a voice for singing. Early childhood is generally good depending on the houses Jupiter rules. Children can bring wealth and opportunities. In a females chart this indicates a wealthy partner. There may be some confusion in early childhood for sometimes this can indicate extremes in certain ways that cause chaos. Money is a value that is taught at an early age. Vision into the future is good and a secure family life is a comfort.

## Saturn

Early home life is difficult with many family problems. The parents may be at odds or just not close. There can be changes in residence with many disruptions early. The voice is underdeveloped due to a lack of respect given for what they say. This will lower the self-esteem. The area of the throat can have many ailments such as sore throats, or thyroid issues. Eating and food become a problem at some stages in life. Money will always be a major issue throughout life, no matter how much is acquired. Depending on the sign there may be large amounts of money gained in a lifetime particularly if Saturn is with Venus or Ketu in Libra. The teeth are strong if Saturn is strong but weak if Saturn is weak. Strong teeth are indicated wit Saturn in Capricorn, Aquarius, and Libra but weak in Leo or Aries.

## Rahu

There is chaos in early childhood creating all sorts of emotional problems throughout life. The parents may be divorced or separated. There will be many ups and downs financially, for wealth and money are an issue to be healed from many lifetimes. Great amounts are gained but with extreme spending lost.

Foods and drink or anything ingested can be a major problem, turning into eating disorders, or addictions like alcoholism, drugs, or smoking. There is an oral fixation. Speech is important and the use of foul language and yelling can get them in trouble.

Aliments with the teeth or eyesight, care must be taken. Social problems come from the disrespect they seem to project.

## Ketu

Losses in childhood seem to influence their lives. Problems in the family such as parent's ill health and financial problems plague early childhood. The stress endured early on creates a great deal of insecurity later in life. No matter how much money is acquired there will always be a sense of lack and insecurity. Financial problems are a source of major concern throughout life.

There are issues around food and drink early that influences the life later. There can be food sensitivities, allergies or aversions. Dental care is important for the teeth may be weak. The eyes are weak and can be very light in color. Speech is delayed but can be a great gift later. They can be good at learning a foreign language.

# Ruler of the 2nd house in the

## 2nd House

Acquisition and Wealth are important and there is great access to acquiring large sums of money. Confidence is strong due to circumstances early in life that empowered or motivated them to gain power.

## 3rd House

Money is made through travel, teaching or writing. The communication skills are solid and the career should involve mass communications as in sales or advertising.

## 4th House

Money and wealth can come from real estate or land. The mother is important in acquisition of property. Security is gained from a solid foundation taught in childhood.

## 5th House

The individual makes their money from all forms of self-expression, creative pursuits, or the ability to be an advisor. They can be excellent in speculation or the stock market.

## 6th House

There is an interest in making money through foods or drink, such as restaurants or anything consumed. Diet and food are of interest and important in health and healing. They can be a nutritionist or a dietician.

## 7th House

Money matters will always be a concern in marriage. The spouse may spend too much or is too materialistic. There can be issues of how money is earned or spent. Fighting over money can break up a marriage.

## 8th House

Financial income comes from other people's money such as investors, investments, insurance or inheritance. Money is made through investments from other people. You have many secrets from early childhood and telling the truth is hard for you.

## 9ᵗʰ House

Finances are taught early in the home and sometimes by the father's role modeling. The father may have some addictive issues. The speech is strong and powerful indicating a career as a teacher or preacher.

## 10ᵗʰ House

The individual makes great money through the profession and career. There is a position of control and leadership in business. They are the spokes person for a company.

## 11ᵗʰ House

This is one of the most powerful placements for wealth and money because the 11ᵗʰ house gives great gains. Money comes in large sums that are from promotions, bonuses or settlements.

## 12ᵗʰ House

Money seems to slip through the hands like water. There is an inability to hold onto money. This can indicate losses financially, or may indicate a generous nature that gives abundantly to others.

## 1ˢᵗ House

This placement brings great wealth, riches and money. This gives a good sense of power and self esteem. They are able to speak clearly what is on their mind.

*Andrew Carnegie* was a Scottish industrialist who made his fortune through the steel industry. He merged two corporations to form the biggest corporation in the world ever, U. S. Steel Co. He married once and had one daughter.

| 6th h. 33 | 7th h. 24 | 8th h. 24 | 9th h. 30 |
|---|---|---|---|
| ♀℞ 21:27 Rev | ☊ 07:40 Kri | ♃ 23:34 Pun | |
| ⛢ 05:12 Dha | Andrew Carnegie<br>Wed 11-25-1835<br>06:00:00<br>Dunfermline<br>United Kingdom<br>Timezone: 0:13:52 DST: 0<br>Latitude: 56N05'00<br>Longitude: 03W28'00<br>Ayanamsha : -21:33:41 Lahiri | | 10th h. 29 |
| ☽ 17:04 Shr<br>♆ 09:57 USh | | | 11th h. 37 |
| | ♇ 07:40 Anu<br>☉ 10:44 Anu<br>♂ 17:35 Jye<br>☿ 23:38 Jye | ♄ 08:42 Swa<br>ASC 20:12 Vis<br>♀ 20:55 Vis | |
| 3rd h. 28 | 2nd h. 26 | 1st h. 24 | 12th h. 29 |

*Chart 7: Andrew Carnegie*

He was a philanthropist donating around 350 million dollars. His quest for education and knowledge initiated the opening of Public Libraries in the U.S.

His 2nd house of money is empowered by four major planets, which have produced this great fortune. Mars is here in its own sign Scorpio magnificently empowering this house and it is with the planet of luxuries, Venus which rules the 1st house meaning the money is brought to him. Also, in this combination the Sun rules the 11th house of great gains.

The most important requirements for wealth are here where both the 2nd house ruler is with the 11th house ruler and they both conjoin the 1st house ruler, All of which means this great fortune is his and all this energy occurs in the house of money, the 2nd house.

As Rahu aspects the Moon this magnifies the Moons power. Rahu in the 8th house of others money gives a wealth of opportunities to work with others with money, plus of course it is aspecting the 2nd house. Ketu the planet that magnifies things as well as Rahu will multiply the ability to expand the power to make money. Particularly because it is next to those three enormously powerful planets for money, Mars, Venus and the Sun, tying in the most powerful houses for money, the 2nd, 1st, and the 11th houses.

*John D. Rockefeller* was an American industrialist and founder of Standard Oil Enterprise; he was the first to make his fortune through the oil business. He was the son of a poverty-ridden con artist. He was an extremely shrewd businessman forcing competitors out of business. He married and had five children. By the time of his retirement in 1902 his fortune was worth over one billion dollars to which he left the majority of to his oldest son, John D. Jr. before his death.

| 12th h. 3? | 1st h. 31 | 2nd h. 23 | 3rd h. 35 |
|---|---|---|---|
| ♀ 26:19 Rev  ☊ 16:05 UBh | ASC 05:27 Ash | ♀ 15:42 Roh  ♂ 24:33 Mrg | ☿ 20:17 Pun  ☉ 24:52 Pun |
| ♅℞ 20:39 PBh | | | |
| ♆℞ 18:02 Shr  ☽ 16:29 Shr | | ♃ 22:45 PPh | |
| ♇℞ 00:49 Vis | | ☋ 16:05 Has | |

John D Rockefeller Sr.
Sun 07-08-1838
23:55:00
Richford, NY,New York
USA
Timezone: 5:04:48 DST: 0
Latitude: 42N21'00
Longitude: 76W12'00
Ayanamsha : -21:36:06 Lahiri

*Chart 8: John D. Rockefeller*

Venus rules the 2nd house (Taurus) and is situated in the 2nd house; it is the ruler of the house and resides there. When Venus is in its sign of ruler ship, either Taurus or Libra or its sign of exaltation, it denotes great wealth and luxuries. Mr. Rockefeller was the richest man in the world and actually the richest man ever if you look at the relative cost of things in his day.

Together in the 2nd house he has the all-powerful Venus with Mars. Mars rules his 1st house (Aries), which means the ruler of the 1st house is with the ruler of the 2nd house of money in the 2nd house. This combination will most definitely bring money to him. Mars aspects the 8th house (ruled by Scorpio) by opposition and since Mars rules Scorpio it empowers it for what the 8th house is good for, which is the ability to acquire money through others. But since Saturn is there in Scorpio these two planets aspecting each other creates a type of persistence that will over ride any opponent. Saturn rules the 11th house of great gains and aspects both Venus and Mars in the 2nd house, so this connects the 11th house ruler with Mars ruler of the 1st (money brought to him) and most importantly the ruler of the 11th house is aspecting the ruler of the 2nd house. Remember, the most powerful influence for money in a chart is when the ruler of the 11th house is connected to the ruler of the 2nd house.

The Lunar Nodes, Rahu and Ketu magnify planets for expansion to create money in a chart. Rahu is aspecting Saturn, which is again the grand ruler of the 11th house of gains, magnifying this ability for gains. Ketu aspects the Moon in the 10th house and also aspects Venus and Mars in the 2nd house. Ketu will magnify a planet in its own sign of rulership (Venus in Taurus) for good results. So it magnifies the power for money and activates planets in earth signs in earth houses (artha). This is a connecting force that brings forth great wealth. The Moon in the 10th house of public recognition produces fame and notoriety in a life. One final note, since he did make his fortune through oil notice he has Neptune, the planet ruling oil, in his 10th house of career tightly conjunct his Moon.

# The 6<sup>th</sup> House: Health and Overcoming Obstacles

*Sow a thought and you reap an action; sow an act and you reap a habit; sow a habit and you reap a character; sow a character and you reap a destiny.*

*Ralph Waldo Emerson 1803-1882*

*The concept of total wellness recognizes that our every thought, word, and behavior affects our greater health and well-being. And we, in turn, are affected not only emotionally but also physically and spiritually.*

*Greg Anderson*

**Satru Bhava:** Health, habits, pets, employees, service, improvement, fitness facilities, food, restaurants, debts, lawsuits, enemies, challenges from competitors, thieves and robberies, police, military, attacks, accidents, acute illnesses, disease, medical profession, intestines.

**Upachaya. Dusthana.**

## Improving Life

This is an upachaya house meaning the capacity to improve and get better in life. It is a house of self-improvement for it is the house that can determine our habits in terms of healthy or unhealthy habits. It rules our health in general and how we take care of ourselves.

Malefic planets are best in the upachaya houses because they give power to improve and get better. One malefic planet in the 6<sup>th</sup> house improves and strengthens the health, but two or more malefic planets in the 6<sup>th</sup> house can destroy health.

## Dusthana and Upachaya

Since it is a dusthana house it has a negative effect for dusthana houses indicate problems, but being an upachaya house with work and diligence obstacles can be overcome.

The 6th house is the house of service and rules over all areas of service and healing professions, such as doctors, nurses, restaurants, flight attendants, firefighters, rehabilitation workers, policemen, waitresses or maids. It involves any service you provide for others. This is the house that gives one the need to want to help others, so it involves councilors and therapist.

## Health

The main meaning of the 6th house is health so it involves the capacity to be fit and healthy but can also be the house of illness and sickness. It represents the immune system and constitution as to illness or disease.

## Nutrition, Diet and Habits

This house indicates nutrition, diet and our daily activities around health and healing. The ability to digest food is of major importance here since it rules the digestive tract of the body. The natal moon in this house can indicate digestive troubles throughout life. Symbolically the ability to digest life's experiences may be challenging as well.

## Work

This is the house of work and enables us to make a living to supply money for our family. But the 10th house is for the career, life's dharma that gives our life purpose and meaning.

The 6th house determines our work as in day-to-day activities of our work. This involves our co-workers, which can make life a joy or misery if we like or don't enjoy working with them. As an upachaya house it can involve a competitive edge with co-workers since this house has a reference to competition.

## Employees

It also rules the people who support us in our work and daily activities, which means our employees. Malefic planets here can indicate bad employees who can cause problems such as thievery or lack of work, possibly leaving the job when you need them most.

## Pets and Animals

Pets and animals come under the rule of the 6th house because they actually do a service for us by protecting our homes and property and providing love and attention.

## Struggles and Lawsuits

This house pertains to difficult situations that require a struggle to overcome. This is the house of enemies, which can come in the form of legal battles such as law suites.

In terms of enemies it may indicate thieves and robberies of your personal property, as well as dishonest employees. Malefic planets here (since this is an upachaya house) will give the ability to fight and win whether it is for a competitive sport, political career or the fight for your life as in healing.

## Accidents

The 6th house karakas are Mars and Saturn therefore this is the house of accidents. So if the problems are not about sickness it could involve accidents.

## Illness and Disease

It is the house of health problems such as illness and disease but since this is the house of overcoming problems this is the house that is known for acute illness and surgery whereas the 8th house is the house of chronic illness, diseases that you cannot get better.

## Debts

This is the house of overcoming financial problems for it deals with debts, which are over come, whereas the 8th house is the house of bankruptcy.

## Relatives, Aunts and Uncles

Relatives come under the domain of this house since it is the 3rd house from the 4th house meaning the brothers or sisters of the mother or the family, the aunts and uncles.

# Bhavat Bhavam

## The Sixth House

### It is the 6th from the 1st

**It is the 1st from the 6th.** The core issue of the 6th house is how we **improve our self** and our life. This entails our health and work. It is the house of service and therefore, pertains to all vocations concerning service. Strong planets here can give a strong constitution or immune system.

**It is the 12th from the 7th house.** This house indicates the end of marriage or possibly the death of the spouse. This is why it will tell of divorce legal battles. It can be the spouse's secrets, thus them being revealed. It is expenditures due to the spouse. This is loss to the second born child.

**It is the 7th from the 12th house.** This would be the enemy of our partners or spouse, as well as our spouse's secrets, denials and shadows.

**It is the 11th from the 8th house.** It is gains from inheritances. The culmination or results from in depth research refer to this house. It is money acquired through taxes or corruption.

**It is the 8th from the 11th house.** This could indicate inheritances or money given from friends. It is death of, or endings to relationships with friends. It may mean the death or inheritances from the eldest sibling as well.

**It is the 10th from the 9th house.** This is the father's career and social standing. It is the results from our spiritual search or studies. It could mean a career in a spiritual field.

**It is the 9th from the 10th house.** This is the house of teaching as a career, or a spiritual career. It is long distance travel for the career. It may represent our boss' father or teacher.

**It is the 5th from the 2nd house.** Advisors on money matters, meaning this can indicate your accountant. This is also advice on foods to eat, so this can represent your nutritionist.

**It is the 2nd from the 5th house.** This will indicate wealth acquired through children, or the wealth of the first-born child. It is the eating habits of our children especially the oldest one.

**It is the 4th from the 3rd house.** This is happiness from your siblings, as well as the security of the youngest sibling or all siblings in general.

**It is the 3rd from the 4th house.** This is the mother's siblings, so it represents the maternal aunts and uncles. It is contracts on real estate and vehicles such as cars. It is your mother's ability to sell herself, her courage and competitive edge.

# Planets in the 6<sup>th</sup> house

## Sun

Strong vitality and health are predicted especially if it is the only malefic here. Focus on heath matters in the area of eating and exercise is a part of the daily regimen. There is a strong interest in healing, directing them to a career as a doctor or nurse. A powerful work ethic and drive to achieve is strong but criticism of others may disturb their position at work. There is the possibility of strong enemies, and lawsuits.

## Moon

Health can fluctuate throughout life, because of sensitivities to many things in the environment. A weak stomach is possible which indicates problems with digestion. Emotions are held in the stomach causing distress and stomach aches. Work is constantly changing and co-workers and employees change often. The mother may be sickly and weak.

## Mercury

Interest in health and healing can lead to a career in teaching, such as a nutritionist. Nervous stress can take its toll on the body. There may be issues with the lungs and a propensity to colds, allergies and asthma. Travel can be a major part of work particularly by car. Service industries or sales can be a good choice for the career.

## Venus

A career that involves beauty products of any kind can bring success. There is an interest in clothing, hair, make-up, or lotions for the body. Relationships for a male can be problematic with conflicts and struggles. For a female the partner can have many secrets and possible health or emotional problems. Coworkers are primarily woman and easy to get along with. Great wealth can come from children.

## Mars

Ambition and drive will build a strong character and body. The muscles are strong and easily developed indicating an interest in sports and bodybuilding. Health can be a concern due to high fevers in early childhood. Employees and coworkers are a problem and may steal or cause mishaps or legal problems. Siblings can cause trouble throughout life, avoid business deals with them. Family businesses cause turmoil with aunts and uncles.

## Jupiter

There is a strong desire to help others and become involved in the healing profession. Humanitarian efforts are near and dear to the heart. A love of animals can direct them to organizations that protect and heal animals. There may be problems of excess in the body, as in too much weight, fluids or congestion. If Jupiter rules difficult houses there can be problems with the liver. Children may have difficulty in health but will produce great money later in life. Blessings come from an extended family with many aunts and uncles.

## Saturn

Discipline and focus on high work ethics and morality is a priority in life. Being on time and organized is important. Problems are expected with employees and coworkers, with no sense of responsibility. Health matters are an essential part of daily living, with a structured daily health regime. Problems with health may be the inspiration to get into better habits. Animals may be a connected to work, like cattle or leather products. Difficulty in marriage leads to periods of seclusion. There is a disconnection or isolation from relatives.

## Rahu

A strong immune system brings robust physical stamina. Matters around health and healing direct the life in an unusual way. There is interest in healing health problems, physical, mental, emotional and spiritual. Ambition and drive in work will give a rise in the chosen profession but problems around coworkers and employees cause conflict. Working with foreigners may bring success. Children become strong after a turbulent childhood.

## Ketu

There is an interest in unusual healing modalities, such as yoga, Ayurveda, herbs or acupuncture. The desire to help those in need can lead to participation in humanitarian group efforts. There may be difficult health problems that are hard to diagnose. Looking at health from a spiritual perspective makes more sense. Love of small animals will bring many pets into the home. Employees and coworkers are undependable and irresponsible. There are many problems for children at an early age.

# Ruler of the 6th house in the

## 6th House

There is a strong physical constitution and interest in health and healing. Work can involve long hours and discipline. The individual is in a job of service and enjoys working for others.

## 7th House

Relationships require understanding and effort to keep together. There are times of conflict and many disagreements. It is not a good idea to work with the spouse. The partner may have many illnesses.

## 8th House

Acute illnesses may be hard to diagnose turning into more serious and chronic disease. There are many surgeries throughout life. Caution and care is required around the work place for there is a risk of accidents or law suits.

## 9th House

Working for the father can be stressful and disadvantageous. The father is weak and feeble and prone to disease. Service as a spiritual student to a guru or any teacher can be counterproductive.

## 10th House

A career in the service industry is well suited. The individual will usually always work for someone else. They are good employees and take their work as a lifelong mission. They need to take care of their knees for they are prone to accidents.

## 11th House

Healing and helping others heal body, mind and spirit takes the individual on a healing journey. The 11th house is the 6th house from the 6th house and will indicate ultimate healing. Friends can be unreliable and troublesome.

## 12th House

Caution around machinery or cars is recommended for this indicates an accident-prone nature. A rewarding career is to work in institutions such as hospitals. Be careful of jealous back stabbing coworkers who talk behind one's back.

## 1st House

Discipline and focus in the area of health will make the individual stronger. Competition increases ambition to get ahead or improve. Attacks around the work place seem to strike when least expected.

## 2nd House

Problems in early childhood may come from ill health and disease. Food and diet can vastly improve the health. There is sensitivity to certain foods. Financial problems concerning debt loom throughout life.

## 3rd House

Conflicts and competition are a source of trouble throughout life with siblings. Siblings are very different and are not compatible. Problems seem to occur when traveling. Education and school are a struggle. There is a strong drive to overcome obstacles.

## 4th House

The mother can be domineering and difficult. Home life is difficult and contentious. The mother may have many illnesses and a difficult life. Real estate and property causes great stress and problems.

## 5th House

Children can have many illnesses and problems. But these health concerns can lead them into the health industry or healing. The mind is troubled, conflicted with worries and pessimism. But the health will be strong.

*Martha Stewart* is the quintessential perfect home maker that has made an empire on food service and catering which is a 6th house profession. She actually branched out in many areas of publishing, merchandising, and television. But in 2004 she was convicted of charges of insider trading and after her prison term made a great comeback and is now just as successful as before. Interestingly enough the 6th house concerns obstacles but is a house of overcoming obstacles, as she most certainly did.

| 6th h. 36 | | 7th h. 27 | | 8th h. 32 | | 9th h. 22 | |
|---|---|---|---|---|---|---|---|
| ♂ 23:15 Rev ☊ 00:31 PBh | ♓ | | ♈ | ☿ 04:15 Kri ♅ 06:51 Kri ♃ 21:46 Roh | ♉ | | ♊ |
| | ♒ | Martha Stewart Sun 08-03-1941 13:33:00 Jersey City, NJ,New Jersey USA | | ☿ 02:22 Pun ♀ 11:04 Pus ☉ 17:55 Asl | ♋ | | 5th h. 26 / 4th h. 26 → 10th h. 23 |
| | ♑ | Timezone: 5 DST: 1 Latitude: 40N43'00 Longitude: 74W04'00 Ayanamsha : -23:02:28 Lahiri | | ♀ 16:06 PPh | ♌ | | 11th h. 24 |
| ☽ 02:22 Mul | ♐ | | ♍ | ASC 17:13 Swa | ♎ | ☊☋ 00:31 UPh ⯝ 02:45 UPh | ♍ |
| 3rd h. 34 | | 2nd h. 24 | | 1st h. 31 | | 12th h. 26 | |

*Chart 9: Martha Stewart*

In her 6th house she has Mars and Ketu in Pisces. Mars rules the 2nd house of how we make our money and the 7th house of partnerships, and Ketu magnifies this energy. Martha did not always have it easy as the 6th house energy suggests. She had many troubles and betrayals through marriage and business partners.

As she went through a very difficult time during her trail for inside trading, the 6th house rules legal battles and Ketu's presence here indicates loss, but with the competitive drive and ambition to overcome obstacles she made a major comeback.

The 6th house rules pets and she is known as a animal lover. She has champion show dogs, cats and horses.

*Emeril Lagasse* is a very famous acclaimed chef. He is probably the most televised Chef in America. He has achieved the highest accolades in television as a chef. His show was recently bought by Martha Stewart for 50 million dollars. In Emeril's chart he has his Moon in the 6th house of the service industry. The Moon, which rules his career house (10th) is in the 6th house of service. The 6th house can indicate healing as in doctors, nurses or nutrition and diet or food.

| 6th h. 31 | 7th h. 26 | 8th h. 24 | 9th h. 31 |
|---|---|---|---|
| ☽ 14:41 UBh<br>☋ 10:44 UBh | ♈ | ♉ | ♊ |
| 5th h. 23 | Emeril Lagasse<br>Thu 10-15-1959<br>07:40:00<br>Fall River, MA, Massachusetts<br>USA<br>Timezone: 5 DST: 1<br>Latitude: 41N42'00<br>Longitude: 71W09'00<br>Ayanamsha : -23:17:43 Lahiri | ♅ 26:57 Asl | 10th h. 35 |
| 4th h. 27 | | ♀ 12:08 Mag<br>♀ 15:06 PPh | 11th h. 38 |
| ♄ 08:27 Mul | ♃ 08:33 Anu | ♂ 02:43 Cht<br>☿ 05:45 Cht<br>♇ 12:49 Swa<br>♀ 16:07 Swa | ☊ 10:44 Has<br>☉ 28:04 Cht |
| 3rd h. 27 | 2nd h. 20 | 1st h. 30 | 12th h. 25 |

*Chart 10: Emeril Lagasse*

There are many indicators of wealth and fortune in this chart. Whenever the 2nd house connects to the 6th house many are drawn to the food industry. The 2nd house deals with how we make our money, but it also rules the mouth, which indicates speech and eating. In this chart the ruler of the 6th house is in the 2nd house, and Emeril has made enormous money from his love of food and his showmanship with his cooking.

He was born under a lunar eclipse with the Sun and Moon opposed with Rahu and Ketu. This will bring the person to the attention of the public through the houses this configuration takes place, and his is in the 6th house of service and the 12th house which rules institutions, such as restaurants. The 12th house usually indicates being behind the scenes, such as the kitchen and privacy.

The Moon individually is the planet of cooking and food, and in the 6th house rules the 10th house of career, fame and social recognition. Plus Jupiter multiplies benefic results from the 2nd house aspecting the Moon in the 6th house of work, service and cooking. Through the profession that these houses, food and cooking has made Emeril a world famous chef.

# The 10<sup>th</sup> House: Career and Purpose

*Learn from the past, set vivid, detailed goals for the future, and live in the only moment of time over which you have any control: now.*

*Denis Waitley*

*"I am not what happened to me, I am what I choose to become.*

*Carl G. Jung*

**Karma Bhava:** Career, social position, fame, honors, purpose, government, authority figures, presidents, bosses, wealth of the father, knees.

**Kendra. Artha.**

## Career

The 10<sup>th</sup> house is an Artha house indicating the ability to make money and provide, but as a Kendra (angle) this house becomes the most powerful house in terms of social standing and gives the ability to be successful in the career. This is the house of one's career. The career in life represents the dharma or purpose in life. Career is an important part of life because this is where we spend most of our time. This house can determine the state of someone's mind since so much time is involved in ones work.

## Noon Time

The 10<sup>th</sup> house represents noontime where the sun is at its highest peak of the day so represents where we are out exposed to the masses or public. This is the house of fame and recognition. The Moon in the 10<sup>th</sup> house can represent fame, because the Moon is the masses of people and the 10<sup>th</sup> house is recognition.

## Leader, Boss or CEO

Our career is where we stand apart from others in our worldly desire to be powerful and strong. The Sun in the 10th house can indicate a leader, boss or CEO in business or owns the business.

## Awards and Achievements

This is the house of the highest awards and achievements in life and indicates the time of recognition, awards, promotions and achievement.

This is the house that indicates our bosses or authority figures, and also represents the government since this is the rulership that dictates or rules over the needs of the country.

## Father's Wealth

In terms of the 9th house being the father, the 10th house represents the father's wealth or money from the father's work. This house can indicate the success of the father.

## Rules Knees and need to Bend

The 10th house and the 10th sign Capricorn rules the knees. The knees are essential in giving mobility. If the knees are injured a person is unable to walk, but the knees also represent flexibility and the need to bend. Those who are stubborn and not flexible will tend to be stifled and not able to grow and move forward in life. This may be the result of a problematic 10th house or planets in Capricorn. Capricorn and the 10th house involve the need to be reverent and humble this is symbolized by the process of kneeling. To be in power but humble is the way of the peaceful warrior.

## Worldly Powers

Planets in this house indicate the power to lead and be in power through ones career, which is of great importance to the worldly powers that control the world.

## Achievement

This is the most powerful house for a sense of achievement and power. It is about our highest sense of achievement, and recognition, notoriety and personal acclaim. It is about achieving our goals through our work, Honors and awards for achievement come when positive planets transit through this house.

# Bhavat Bhavam

## The Tenth House

### It is 10th from the 1st .

**It is the 1st from the 10th.** The core meaning of the 10th house is our sense of achievement and this usually comes through a career or profession that gives a sense of **purpose**. This is the house of our public or social standing in the world. It is the house of fame, being publicized for the work you have achieved. A life well lived needs to have a sense of purpose. If there is no sense of purpose in life, life seems meaningless and this void leads to depression. Finding meaning and purpose in life gives a sense of your dharma and overthrows difficult karma. This is the house of the sum accumulation of our efforts working towards a goal.

**It is the 12th from the 11th house.** This is the house of losses from the eldest sibling. It can indicate expenditure on friends.

**It is the 11th from the 12th house.** This house can indicate large sums of money from charities or government grants.

**It is the 9th from the 2nd house.** This is the house of speakers and speaking truth.

**It is the 2nd from the 9th house.** This is the house of wealth and money made from speaking especially about spirituality. It indicates our father's wealth or worth.

**It is the 8th from the 3rd house.** It is the death of our siblings or our courage.

**It is the 3rd from the 8th house.** This can indicate ambition relating to a deep competitive drive.

**It is the 7th from the 4th house.** It is our mother's spouse therefore; this house indicates how our mother relates to our father.

**It is the 4th from the 7th house.** This indicates the fixed assets such as real estate owned by the spouse. It is our mother-in-law, for it is our spouse's mother. It may indicate the happiness and security of our spouse. This may all be relative to a business partner as well as the spouse.

**It is the 6th from the 5th house.** This is the house of our children's health. It is how hard our children work. This especially pertains to our first-born child.

**It is the 5th from the 6th house.** This is advice given that is healing, as in therapy or counseling.

# Planets in the 10th house

### Sun

The Sun works best in the 10th house where it gives a sense of power and good career opportunities. This placement indicates the power to be the boss, CEO, or have ownership in business. It is hard to work or take orders from others, with a sense of ownership. They should own their own business. The father has an influence over the career choice. They have strong self-esteem and confidence.

### Moon

The Moon represents the public and this placement can indicate fame or recognition. This is usually an indication of success through the career. Dominate or influential people in life may be women or the boss may be a woman. The mother may be a leader or is successful. A career in a field of service can bring personal satisfaction or a job with the government. There is a good connection to the mother-in-law.

### Mercury

A career in communications such as public relations or advertising will bring success. Traveling may be a part of work. They are gifted in connecting people in the business world through communications. Professions as a writer, speaker or teacher are indicated. The mother-in-law can offer valuable information. The father is youthful with a great sense of humor.

### Venus

A career using creativity brings success, such as design in fashion, beauty, home decoration or the arts, Success and recognition will come from a powerful career, known for beauty, grace and charm. Venus is fortunate in the 10th house and indicates wealth and money from the career. In a males chart he could meet his wife at work. Wealth may come from a successful father. Venus in Pisces, Libra or Taurus will bring success and wealth in the career. Wealth comes from the mother-in-law.

## Mars

Career success comes from strong ambition and drive. Mars in Aries, Scorpio or Capricorn gives early success in the career. They are leaders and know how to give direction. The father had a very difficult beginning, and caused contention and problems in the home. Family discord may have lead to divorce. The mother-in-law causes problems with the family and home life.

## Jupiter

Career success comes easy due to empowerment from family, especially the father. A successful father set the example and gives opportunities. Family businesses may be handed down to the children. This indicates a prominent position with great authority and talents in teaching and leading especially when Jupiter is in Scorpio, Aries, or Pisces. A secure family brings happiness. The mother-in-law is loving and accepting within the family.

## Saturn

Career success comes from hard work, discipline and experience. A long-standing career comes from diligence and persistence. The father is a self made man who came from a life of struggles. He is a serious hard workingman with high unattainable expectations. He was not there emotionally. The outlook on life is to work hard with no breaks and nothing comes easy. The mother-in-law is detached and hard to get along with.

## Rahu

Drive and power bring high success quickly but there are many consequences along the way. Success comes from an unusual career. There is a power that comes from a deep-seated insecurity to prove thy self. The message in childhood was that we are nothing without money and dedication to hard work, which is the only way to achieve self-respect and self worth. The father may have addictions, such as alcohol and was difficult towards the mother Family discord plagued early childhood. The mother-in-law is excessive in many ways.

## Ketu

A very unusual career is preferred, not confined to an office, freedom and change is essential. Changes in work or career are common for there seems to be something always missing in the area of work. The changes are due to a search to find a career that is fulfilling, but that quest never seems to be fulfilled. They are forever searching for a career of passion. There is sadness that comes from the father's childhood that makes one want seek a career to help others. He never achieved his goals and felt life was not satisfying. A dissatisfaction of life originates from this childhood experience.

# Ruler of the 10th house in the

### 10th House

Career success is a driving force in life and consumes most of the time and thoughts. They are a leader and command respect in the work place. The profession defines and labels the person.

### 11th House

They know very influential people from work who can give opportunities and support. Great gains and wealth come from the career. Social events can bring great political connections.

### 12th House

The career involves work behind the scenes such as large institutions like hospitals or government offices. Changes in work may come from reorganization or takeovers. Charities and a need to help others are indicated as a career.

### 1st House

Success from the career defines and gives a sense of self-esteem. They determine and have a sense of self through their work. Strength and fortitude give a healthy body. As a leader they attract many followers.

### 2nd House

A successful career brings wealth and money. Life was planned from an early age to succeed in attaining security through financial planning. Banking, loans dealing with money are good career choices.

### 3<sup>rd</sup> House

A career in the communications field such as public relations, advertising, or sales brings success. Education, teaching, traveling and writing are a part of work. Working with computers and the Internet are a major part of the career.

### 4<sup>th</sup> House

Working with real estate in sales, renovation or Interior design will bring success and financial wealth. There may be an interest in the area of loans for property. Working from the home can be a lucrative business.

### 5<sup>th</sup> House

Working with children can be an interest in career. Financial gains may come from speculation such as investing in the stock market. Entertainers and businesses involving entertainment are a drive and passion.

### 6<sup>th</sup> House

Career in the health field such as doctors or nurses is indicated. Businesses that involve the service industry are desired like restaurants or hotels. Finding work for others like employment agencies and headhunters come under this placement.

### 7<sup>th</sup> House

Working with the spouse brings career success, or the spouse may come through the career. They could be in the same type of work. Business partners will bring an advantage to your work.

### 8<sup>th</sup> House

A career in investigation such as private investigators or police work is preferable. Scientific research can be mentally stimulating. Psychoanalysis in the field of psychology satisfies the need to understand things. Problem solvers for companies have this placement.

### 9<sup>th</sup> House

There is a desire to be a part of academics as in teaching college or University professor. Publishing, law or spiritual teachings will be a major part of life. The father or a teacher had a positive influence on life and career direction.

*John F. Kennedy* was the 35th President of the United States of America. He was inaugurated as President January 20th, 1961 and assassinated November 22nd, 1963. He was one of the most charismatic Presidents and was suspected as having affairs with Hollywood movie stars. But he achieved great accomplishments with civil rights in America. He was a fighter and a great leader creating great changes in transformational times.

| 7th h. 32 | 8th h. 24 | 9th h. 24 | 10th h. 29 |
|---|---|---|---|
| ♄ | ♈ | ♂ 00:20 Kri | ♊ |
| | ♂ 25:43 Bha | ☉ 15:08 Roh | ♀ 10:33 Ard |
| | ☿ 27:53 Kri | ♀ 24:02 Mrg | ☊ 18:32 Ard |
| 6th h. 38 ♒ | | John F. Sr. Kennedy | ♋ 11th h. 24 |
| ♅℞ 01:00 Dha | | Tue 05-29-1917 | ♃ 04:27 Pus |
| | | 15:00:00 | ♆ 09:57 Pus |
| 5th h. 30 ♑ | | Brookline | ♌ 12th h. 22 |
| | | USA | |
| | | Timezone: 5 DST: 0 | ☽ 24:30 PPh |
| | | Latitude: 42N19'54 | |
| | | Longitude: 71W07'18 | |
| | | Ayanamsha : -22:42:29 Lahiri | |
| ♐ | ♍ | ♏ | ♍ |
| ☋ 18:32 PSh | | | ASC 27:17 Cht |
| 4th h. 31 | 3rd h. 25 | 2nd h. 28 | 1st h. 30 |

*Chart 11: John F. Kennedy*

His family seemed to be under a curse with tragedy after tragedy. His older brother Joseph was killed in WWII 1944, his older sister Kathleen died later in a plane crash in France1948, his mentally retarded sister was operated on and died, and his wife Jacqueline had two still born babies one in 1956, and another in 1963 while in the White House. John F Kennedy was assassinated 1963 and his brother Robert Kennedy was assassinated 1968, his youngest brother Ted survived a plane crash where the pilot and aides died 1964 and a car crash 1969 that produced a scandal Ted never overcame and then his son John Kennedy JR was killed in a plane crash in 1999.

Aside from such great loss the place of his greatest achievement was the Presidency of the United States where he will go down in history forever. The 10th house is the house of Presidents, kings and rulers.

President Kennedy has Ketu in his 10th house indicating transformational change. He did great things to change the world but the career he chose brought him great loss. For this is an indication of his assassination.

As Ketu the indicator of loss is in Gemini, Mercury ruler of Gemini and the 10th house is in the 8th house of death. Mercury is with Mars in the 8th house, both in Aries and Mars rules the 8th house of death.

This is a very ominous chart for life and death but does indicate a life of surrender and empowerment for the world. He sacrificed his life for the betterment of humanity.

*Napoleon Bonaparte* was the emperor of France and regarded as one of the greatest military commanders of all time. He was responsible for overthrowing many Ancient Regime type monarchies in Europe and spreading official values of the French Revolution to other countries.

*Chart 12: Napoleon Bonaparte*

Napoleon Bonaparte had great leadership abilities with a powerful 10th house, the house of kings, leaders and fame. He is an Icon and will be forever remembered in history.

He has both Saturn and Mercury in the 10th house. Mercury indicates the mind and intelligence and with Saturn the planet of responsibility, order and discipline indicates the ability to plan and instigate his military commands. Saturn his yoga karaka planet is his most powerful planet in his chart rules the 4th and 5th houses. The 4th house indicates protection of the home while the 5th house rules intelligence. His talent as a world leader and commander came from his great ability to create strategic plans.

Mercury as ruler of the 9th and 11th hoses gave him blessings and fortune to bring success to his command.

The Moon as ruler of his 10th house is placed in the 4th house and aspects the 10th house that it rules. This indicates great fame and recognition for his great work and leadership. The Moon is the public and the masses and its association to the 10<sup>th</sup> house is very powerful. Plus Saturn and the Moon are in each other's signs, Saturn in Cancer and Moon in Capricorn further indicating greatness and power. This is a chart of power, fame, mental focus and achievement with these planets influencing this house of leadership and kings.

# Part III

# Air Triplicity - Kama Houses
## 3rd House, 7th House, 11th House

*It is a rare person who wants to hear what he doesn't want to hear.*

*Dick Cavett*

### Upachaya Houses

The 3rd house is an upachaya house meaning it is a growing house where things get better over time. It is a house of improvement, urging a continual quest to make things better, and this is where the competitive edge comes in. The 6th, 11th, and some say the 10th, are also upachaya houses and all give a drive for improvement.

The 3rd and the 11th are kama houses. The kama houses (3, 7, and 11) are the houses of desire; a part of their quest to achieve goals. From my observation the houses most prominent for invincible willpower, ambition and drive are the upachaya houses 3, 6 and 11.

The 11th is the ultimate house of desire and the achievement of one's desires. It is the house of great gains, and that is exactly what it promises, the great gain of one's desires. The 11th is the 6th house from the 6th and will also indicate any health issues that result in healing. This will be revealed through the example chart I have chosen to prove this point.

## Air Triplicity

The air triangle is concerned with how we connect to others. It is comprised of houses 3, 7, and 11 and relates to the signs Gemini, Libra, and Aquarius. The yearning for relationship is part of our desire body. An integral aspect of relationship is how we convey our information, i.e. the art of communication. The need to be understood and reinforced in our feelings and ideas gives us a feeling of completion.

The 3$^{rd}$ house and sign Gemini is about conveying information, and receiving thoughts and ideas. It is the house of communication and learning. It rules our early relationships in life, especially our siblings. In fact, these early relationships initiate our ways of relating to other people, which often includes a degree of competition.

The 7$^{th}$ house and sign Libra is about the one-on-one relationships, which make up our commitments. It is about learning to share. Most especially, it is about sharing your life with another. Sharing takes a certain amount of compromise and balancing. Relationships give us a sense of wholeness and completion, in the sense that someone understands and supports us. This is a need and desire that validates our feelings.

The 11$^{th}$ house and sign Aquarius is about our ultimate desires. It involves our hopes and wishes. In terms of our relationships, these are things we usually share with our friends. Friendships put us in touch with community. The 11$^{th}$ house and sign bring out our humanitarianism, i.e. our desire to be in touch with the greater whole of humankind. This includes groups and organizations where people can feel connected and share common interests.

The air triplicity conveys our ideas, needs, and desires through relationships. These relationships begin in early childhood.

Sharing starts with our siblings (3$^{rd}$ house) and later we need a lifelong partnership (7$^{th}$ house). Our need to feel connected to friends and groups (11$^{th}$ house) fulfills our need to know we are not alone. These are the kama houses – the houses of desire and relationship.

The kama houses are 3, 7 and 11. They relate to the three air signs (air triplicity). The 3rd house relates to the first air sign Gemini, the 7th Libra, and the 11th Aquarius. These houses define how we convey our ideas, needs, and desires through relationships. The 3rd house describes our early relationships in which we learn by sharing with our siblings. The 7th is the need of a lifelong partnership. The 11th is the desire to feel connected to friends and groups or organizations.

The air element is about desires. These manifest in the form of thinking, relating, and communicating. Gemini is the first air sign; five signs away is Libra, and nine signs away from Gemini is Aquarius. These three signs are called the air triplicity. They deal with ways of communicating our thoughts, and our relationships in life. Houses 3, 7, and 11 relate to air. These are called the kama houses.

The air triplicity conveys our ideas, needs, and desires through relationships. These relationships begin in early childhood.

- Sharing starts with our siblings (3rd house), and
- Later we need a lifelong partnership (7th house).
- Our need to feel connected to friends and groups (11th house) fulfills our need to know we are not alone.

These are the kama houses – the houses of desire and relationship.

# The 3rd House: Will Power and Communications

*The one thing over which you have absolute control is your own thoughts.*
*It is this that puts you in a position to control your own destiny.*

*Paul G. Thomas*

**Sahaja Bhava:** Courage, life force, arts of all kinds, theater, directors, painting, drawing, music, writing, sports, travel, hobbies, father-in-law, younger siblings, sibling rivalry, lower education, success through own efforts, initiative, motivation, adventures, competition, sales, voice, all forms of communication, hearing in general and the right ear in particular, hands, shoulders arms, and lungs.

**Upachaya. Kama.**

## Willpower

The house most indicated for willpower and courage is the third, often one of the most overlooked of houses. It is not usually involved in any important yogas, yet it is the house that gives the most power for change. It is the house of competition where malefic planets, especially Mars, can deliver more drive to accomplish one's goals. The 3rd house from the Moon (Chandra lagna) will reveal just as much and must always be assessed.

The 3rd house is a powerhouse meaning it deals with the ability to make things happen through pure raw will power. Will power has to come from a burning drive and desire felt deep within. Interestingly it is a part of the air element, which reflects the power of the thinking mind. Everything initiates with a thought and the ability to manifest anything in the material world comes from the power to activate and act on a thought. Once the thought is put into action it takes the power of communication to project the creation out into the world. It takes others to bring projects into manifestation. It is the act of sharing information that brings people together and the Kama houses are about relationships and the air triplicity concerns communications. In sharing our thoughts and ideas we are initiating the process of creation.

## Need to Express Ideas

The basis of the Kama houses are said to be desire. Creating things is meaningless if we are unable to share them with others. These houses are based on the aspect of a burning need to express ones' ideas with others, to share and experience. We need others to experience love. This is a part of extending our feelings. The burning need to extend and share our feelings is the energy of the $3^{rd}$ house. This is a necessary and essential component of living life to be able to share. If we are unable to share there is a missing piece of the process of life. If this piece is missing it results in depression. Loneliness and isolation manifests into depression, which is based on no sense of purpose.

## Teaching

Teaching is a $3^{rd}$ house matter and through the power of teaching we share our information and connect through the mind to others. In the process of teaching we are empowering others, which is a true sense of real power. This is the power felt through sharing, giving. This is an act of selflessness and it inspires one in a way that gives joy and happiness. Extending oneself in this manner gives a sense of connection and completion, which gives back to the self with a true sense of accomplishment, living a life with meaning and purpose.

## Depression and no Meaning in Life

The $3^{rd}$ house can give the sense of meaning and purpose when ideas are shared that are beneficial to both involved especially in the process of teaching. But when there is no connect to others through sharing a feeling of isolation and loneness is felt equating to a sense of depression. Depression is a sense of no meaning or purpose in life.

## Thoughts

Ideas are fleeting and can change throughout the day. They are a process of the mind. The process of the mind with where thoughts come from and where how they affect the person and their life is relative to a person's environment.

Where do thoughts come from and how does the mind work? This is a mystery to all. But it is definitely the process of the 3$^{rd}$ house and Mercury.

## Mercury

Mercury rules the 3$^{rd}$ sign Gemini, which is relative to the 3$^{rd}$ house. To investigate where thoughts come from and why they come and go in a fleeting manor is to understand Mercury. Mercury is the fastest moving planet and from our vantage point on Earth it appears to travel with the Sun. This can indicate the fast movement of the thought process by the fast speed of Mercury but the fact that it appears to travel with the Sun can symbolize that the mind is very ego centered. In other words our minds are always based on our own perceptions of the self. It can also mean we are connected to the giver of life, the Sun, which means essentially we are a part of the Divine and we can never really separate from this Divine connection.

## Beliefs are Formed at an Early Age

In the thinking process the mind and our beliefs are formed at an early age based on the conditions and experiences recorded. As babies we observe everything as experiential and these recordings become the tapes that are replayed throughout our lives activating our unconscious reactions to life's stimulus. Our first experiences in relationships as children have a huge part in how we disseminate information throughout our life.

This takes into account, our early environment, home, family, culture, parents, siblings, birth order, school, both social and learning, neighborhoods, socio economics and religion. All these areas as to how they have an effect on our mind and consciousness in childhood are actually a part of the 3$^{rd}$ house. So it is these tapes that are instilled in the mind that conditions how we respond to events throughout life and are revealed through the 3$^{rd}$ house.

## Competition

Many of these early matters have a quality of competition or a competitive edge for the way we fight for the attention of our parents with our siblings becomes a part of our conditioning. The drive to compete with others in any area is seen through this process. This can be the competitive force in school academics or in sports, which are other 3$^{rd}$ house matters.

Thoughts come from the stimulus in daily matters; things we are exposed to or see activate the mind and the thoughts. We see outward stimulus in our daily activities, but the thoughts we have concerning what we see is colored through the lenses of our past experiences. We all see something different from our own personal past relationships and experiences.

## Thoughts as Wavelengths

What we see directs our consciousness and what we think about. If we see someone who my look like a friend we know, then our thoughts begin to think about this friend and experiences we may have shared with them in a fleeting thought. Then surprisingly the friend may call that day. How does this all work?

First thoughts are things and they are put out as wavelengths in the air (air signs work this way). It is much like radio waves that are perceived and picked up by others. But why did the person that reminded us of this person come across our path that day?

This is a part of the divine order of things that connects us all but is a part of the mysterious workings of the Universe. This is the science of astrology as the planets direct these forces in our lives.

## Opening the Mind

But in the process to expose ourselves to the stimulus that we have never seen or experienced before can be a stimulus to open and change previous perceptions. This is the experience that traveling can give, especially to other cultures and countries. Travel is a learning experience that opens the mind and this is another 3rd house matter.

## Mercury the Messenger

Mercury in Greek mythology is the only god by being the messenger that could go in and out of the underworld. This can symbolize many things, one that our minds can travel anywhere without the physical body, and that our consciousness never dies. We will always exist though the consciousness that is represented through our minds. This is indication that we exist without our physical body and that we are our consciousness.

## Androgyny

Our eternal being like Mercury has no gender and is the planet of eternal youth because in reality our soul does not grow old. There is no such thing as time or the duality of gender. In both Greek and Indian mythology Mercury pertains to androgyny.

## Change the Mind and Change the Life

The mind is our most precious resource and gives us the ability to learn and grow. If we can change the way we think we can change our world. This revolves around our will. The will is conditioned by our thoughts. This will determine the outcome of our life.

Another specific matter dealing with the 3rd house is the ears and hearing. The need to be herd is very important and the senses of being not hear can be stifling for a child and will be reflected throughout life as a sense of meaninglessness. They will believe they are worthless and relinquish their expression and turn inward experiencing depression.

## The Need to be Heard

When someone is discounted, they feel unheard which creates many insecurities and anger. People need to be heard. This relates to many core issues pertaining to the mind and even mental disorders or bad behavior.

## Mental Disorders

Many mental disorders originate from the sense of being discounted throughout life. This is the root of most mental disease and depression for people feel a sense of depression from feeling rejected and oppressed. No self-esteem comes from being discounted. A sense of worthlessness with sense of purpose destroys a life.

## Siblings

Mars is the karaka (indicator) of the 3rd house and siblings. This brings forth the power of Mars pertaining to this house. Mars is the indicator for siblings, but Mars in the 3rd house will cause problems with siblings. There is too much competition with them and it never gets resolved. Mars in this house gives great drive producing a great athlete.

## Duality Twins and Breath

Since Mercury and Gemini deal with dual (two) or twins it represents the organs or body parts in pairs, such as the lungs, arms and hands of the upper body. It gives the power of breath and life and this is a reason the 3$^{rd}$ house deals with courage, and life. It is a house accessed for longevity, mainly because it gives drive and desire to live and enjoy life. It is when we take our first breath that life begins. And when we take our last breath that our life ends.

## Creativity Self Expression and Writing

Since it rules the hands and it is a house of creating. This is the house of writing and self-expression through this form of communication. Interestingly the 5$^{th}$ house is the 3$^{rd}$ house from the 3$^{rd}$ house and is thought of as the main house of creativity, but this is because it is a dharma house pertaining to fire which pushes outward creativity in a purposeful meaningful way full of fire and inspiration.

## Communications

The 3$^{rd}$ house is the initiator of creativity through the mind, thoughts and action and this comes through communications as well. The arts are a form of communication as in drawing, painting, music, writing, dancing or drama. They say a picture is worth a thousand words. The 3$^{rd}$ house is creativity, particularly using the hands.

## Sales, Internet, Television, Radio and Computers

It deals with sales and passing on of products and information. The word mercantile comes from Mercury. This is another way of distributing things and ideas. The 3$^{rd}$ house and Mercury rule all forms of communication therefore it rules the internet, television, radio, and computers which a major component of our society today. If any of these ways of connecting stopped our entire world would go down.

There would be no way to make money or to connect which activates the world. To connect to others, it is the purpose of being on earth. People must connect to share and thrive. The 3$^{rd}$ house is of major importance to life and existence.

## The Creative Process

A burning need and inspiration is initiated by fire, to make something a reality in the material world is a part of earth, to share with others is air and the release of emotion is water. This is the process of the four aims of life, Dharma, Artha, Kama and Moksha.

The power of three begins the creative process.

# Bhavat Bhavam

## The Third House

**It is the 3rd from the 1st .**

**It is the 1st from the 3rd.** The core meaning of the 3rd house is **communications,** getting information across. It is our communicative skills of all kinds particularly with writing. Communications today involve television, radio, mail, computers and the Internet. Since the 3rd house rules the hands this insinuates writing and skills like crafts and hobbies. It rules all forms of the arts such as painting, sculpture, sewing, theatre and music. It is short travels particularly by car. It is our will power, courage and competitive drive. Last but not least, our siblings, especially the youngest one.

**It is the 2nd from the 2nd house.** It is the ability to provide and acquire our own earned money, our sense of self worth, and how you make money.

**It is the 8th from the 8th house.** This is another prominent house for death. It can indicate our chronic illnesses. This house will give clues as to what we die from. It may be a house of disgrace too. It indicates interest in life after death. It can be extremely metaphysical.

**It is the 4th from the 12th house.** This house can indicate living in a foreign country. It can be assets from other people's losses, such as estate sales, pawn shops, repossessed cars and homes.

**It is the 12th from the 4th house.** It is the endings or death of the parents, the past and security. It is the house of the death of the mother, and possibly the end of happiness.

**It is the 5th from the 11th house.** It is love and advice from our friends, and our heart's desires. It can be gains and wealth given from our children.

**It is the 11th from the 5th house.** This is your oldest child's success and friends. It is wealth from speculation or the stock market.

**It is the 6<sup>th</sup> from the 10<sup>th</sup> house.** It is working in a career with health or health products. It is hard work and achievement from our careers or the conditions in the work place. It represents the health or retirement of our boss. It may even be a career or work with pets or animals, such as a veterinarian.

**It is the 10<sup>th</sup> from the 6<sup>th</sup> house.** It can represent careers that develop from jobs, for example a waiter in a restaurant moving up to management or ownership. It is your social standing and reputation at work.

**It is the 7<sup>th</sup> from the 9<sup>th</sup> house.** This is our father's perception of his spouse, (our mother). It may also indicate partnerships with teachers, professors or gurus.

**It is the 9<sup>th</sup> from the 7<sup>th</sup> house.** This house indicates our spouse's spirituality and beliefs, including religious beliefs. Their beliefs will condition the luck or fortune they allow. It is also our spouse's father and our partner's higher education and travels.

## Planets in the 3<sup>rd</sup> house

### Sun

Sun indicates courage and ambition. Communication skills are highly developed and an important part of life. The work involves computers and Internet skills. There are creative gifts using the hands, as with crafts, hair cutting, knitting, pottery, woodworking or being handy around the house. But one the most important skills attributed here is writing, such as articles, books, songs, or contracts. The Sun is male energy and indicates brothers, or being and only child or the youngest family member, especially if the Sun is in Aries or Leo. Traveling and sales are a part of work and the father may be in a line of sales. There may be a problem with hearing.

### Moon

Traveling is a major part of life, constantly going places, with adaptability moving along with new trends. Writing and communication skills are developed. There is a quest for knowledge, always learning and are avid readers. Gossiping is irresistible and unavoidable, and known to be a good listener. The Moon is female energy indicating sisters and may be the youngest in the family. There is a need to move through music and love to dance and perform in the early part of life.

## Mercury

Traveling for work keeps one on the road. With extremely convincing ways can make a great living in sales. Very crafty and talented in many ways, gives wide range knowledge of many things, can be a trivia buff. Mercury is youth and may indicate the youngest one in the family or a large range of years between siblings. Close association and communications with the neighbors. With highly developed communication skills there is talent with learning languages.

## Venus

Creativity is a gift with an eye for color and design and the knowhow to decorate or make things beautiful. A love for the arts gives an aptitude to understand and appreciate art. Understanding of the creative process and love of art may indicate a curator or appraiser of paintings or in an artistic field. Music moves the soul and inspires the appreciation of music or can indicate musical abilities. A talented creative younger sister influences the life. A sale as in a line of clothing or beauty products is a good career choice.

## Mars

Competition drives ambition to compete and win at all costs. Physical strength and strong developed muscles direct life in the field of sports and athletics. Mars in Capricorn, Aries or Scorpio gives a strong competitive drive and makes great athletes. There are major issues and problems with siblings particularly brothers. Fighting and conflict usually drives a split in the relationship. Neighbors are aggravating causing problems.

## Jupiter

All forms of creativity come natural. In the early years the performing arts such as dance is an important way of expression. But in the later years communication skills are developed in writing. The 3rd house is about writing shorter articles while the 5th house (3rd from the 3rd) is about writing books. Teaching is a way of life and will find a way to teach anything and everything. There will be extensive travel far and wide throughout the lifetime. Generally indicates the youngest one in the family, and will have more than one sibling, or a large family.

## Saturn

Serious focus and a deep responsibility to express in a meaningful way give direction into a field of communications using the written word. Saturn gives discipline and persistence to write a book. Intense focus can tune out the constant chatter from others. There are problems with hearing or the ears in early life. It also indicates an only child or disconnection or nothing in common with siblings, possibly because of a large age gap or distant locations. Education and school in early life proved difficult, maybe trouble with peers or teachers. Learning is hard initially but through discipline can master certain subjects.

## Rahu

Talent with computers is a means of interaction and skill. Can teach others technology with an ability to understand the electronic world. Understanding of technology gives the ability to make a great living. Work is around unusual people or foreigners. There can be very complicated relationship with siblings with a split at some point in life. Siblings may be half sisters or brothers. Early life was difficult in terms of education and making friends due to many changes of schools while growing up. Problems with the ears are an issue in childhood.

## Ketu

Losses around siblings create an empty void in the early life. There can be a sibling that dies or has some kind of emotional or physical problem. As an only child there is a yearning for siblings throughout life. Early education and learning may have been extremely difficult, but a specific talent is developed and gives life meaning. This placement indicates a different way of learning, such as dyslexia, but extremely creative and able to think outside the box. There is a quest to travel the world but can never seem to find what they are looking for, finally realizing the answers are inside instead of outside.

# Ruler of the 3rd house in the

### 3rd House

Competition inspires drive and ambition. Communication skills are highly developed. There is an interest in all forms of creativity but writing as a form or self-expression, teaching and learning are a way of life. Excelling in early education and they have a love of reading and learning throughout life.

## 4<sup>th</sup> House

Close family ties give a sense of community and security throughout life. The mother can be very creative and intelligent instilling the importance of education. They are very crafty renovating and building always fixing things around the house.

## 5<sup>th</sup> House

This is a sign of a very skilled writer. The ability to create is very pronounced. There is a need for self-expression and mastery in a particular field. They have intelligent, creative and very unique children. Superior communication skills are developed in later life.

## 6<sup>th</sup> House

Difficult relations with siblings come about from struggles in early life. Learning and school is a choir and hard work is required to complete the education. Interest in health matters such as nutrition and diet are of interest throughout life.

## 7<sup>th</sup> House

The spouse is met through school or education, or marriage is to a childhood sweet heart or someone from early life. Communications is the most important part of relationships with someone open minded and educated.

## 8<sup>th</sup> House

Difficult relationships with a sibling can cause early trauma, and in extreme cases the death of a sibling. Siblings do not prosper throughout life and go their separate ways. There is an intense interest in life after death and metaphysical subjects.

## 9<sup>th</sup> House

World travel opens the mind to an open-minded perspective to the world. Life revolves around learning, traveling and teaching. As a publisher information is spread worldwide. The father is an inspiration and encourages education.

## 10<sup>th</sup> House

The field of communications will always be of interest and promotes the choice of career. Advertising, public relations, Internet, and the social media constitute many gifts. Great at sales this indicates the ability to sell thyself.

## 11th House

Indicates the oldest and the youngest therefore the only born in the family. Friends are the most important connection and are a support system throughout life. Success is indicated through sales or communication skills.

## 12th House

Travels to foreign countries are essential in the field of sales. As an international traveler there is great interest in other cultures. Siblings are separated in early life. They may be very different with no emotional connection or live far away. There is a sense of loss around siblings. The competitive drive is lost at an early age.

## 1st House

Competitive drive is acquired at an early age but the initial start in life was difficult. Confidence is gained through difficulty. There is an understanding of the power and art of communication and learn to develop these skills early.

## 2nd House

A living is made on talent and in the field of communication. The pursuit of writing, speaking, teaching, and traveling are a lifestyle. Books, articles and song writing bring out the need to express through creativity. Speaking is just as powerful as the written word.

*Stephen King* is a prolific writer and screenwriter. As a former English teacher he achieved amazing notoriety. He wrote 40 successful horror novels by 1999, 26 movies were made from his books. He has grossed more than 100 million dollars per year. His books have sold over 100 million copies in 33 languages.

*Chart 13: Stephen King*

In terms of a career the 3rd house is the house of communications and a profession pertaining to writing. The 5th house is the house of talent and since the 5th house is the 3rd house from the 3rd house this indicates it is also a house for writing talents. Actually, the 5th house can mean writing books while the 3rd house is simply all-writing ventures. Both houses together with powerful planets definitely point to a successful writer.

Focusing in on his 3rd house of communications and writing he has Mercury in its exalted sign Virgo. Mercury is placed next to mystical dreamy Neptune giving his writing deep imagination. Venus in the 3rd house is a bit weak in Virgo, but when a planet is debilitated with a planet that is exalted the weak planet is strengthened from the support of the exalted planet. Venus is ruler of the 11th house of great gains in the 3rd house of writing, plus the Sun ruler of the 2nd house is in the 3rd house with the 11th house ruler, Venus. Here is a great combination of both planets ruling the most important money houses 2 and 11 with exalted Mercury, which just so happens to be the ruler of the 3rd house placed in the 3rd house. This is a dynamite combination of success, wealth and money through writing.

His 5<sup>th</sup> house is occupied by Jupiter with Ketu, giving him great depth with an enormously creative intellectual mind. The 5<sup>th</sup> house is the 3<sup>rd</sup> house from the 3<sup>rd</sup> house indicating writing books. Jupiter rules his 9<sup>th</sup> house and resides in the 5<sup>th</sup> house of the mind and intelligence empowering his luck, fortune and talents. Additionally, his Mars and Moon are exchanged by being in each other's signs. This is a mutual reception, plus Jupiter aspects the Moon, Mars and Saturn. This connects the 1<sup>st</sup>, 5<sup>th</sup> and 9<sup>th</sup> houses, these are the houses of inspiration and luck. This is truly an amazing chart depicting this man's incredible writing skills, talents, mental qualities and the opportunities to get them out in the world for his ultimate success.

*Tiger Woods* has achieved the highest acclaim for golf in U.S. history to date. He is one of the most successful and highest paid athletes of our time. In the year 2000 he won all four championships, the Masters, the US Open, the British Open and the PGA. In 1997 he signed endorsements for Nike and Titleist for over 60 million dollars for over 5 years. Currently his fortune has grown to over the billionaire mark.

| 7th h. 28 | | 8th h. 22 | | 9th h. 26 | | 10th h. 29 | |
|---|---|---|---|---|---|---|---|
| ♃ 21:57 Rev | ♓ | ☋ 27:24 Kri | ♈ | ♂ ℞ 24:02 Mrg | ♉ | | ♊ |
| ♒ | | Tiger Woods | | | | | ♋ |
| ☿ 02:54 USh | ♑ | Tue 12-30-1975 22:50:00 Long Beach, CA,California USA Timezone: 8 DST: 0 Latitude: 33N46'01 Longitude: 118W11'18 Ayanamsha : -23:31:32 Lahiri | | | | ♄ ℞ 07:35 Pus | |
| ☉ 15:26 PSh | ♐ | ♀ 05:00 Anu ♅ 18:58 Jye ☽ 28:51 Jye | ♏ | ♆ 12:49 Swa ☊ 27:24 Vis | ♎ | ASC 00:53 UPh ♀ 18:07 Has | ♍ |
| 4th h. 28 | | 3rd h. 28 | | 2nd h. 30 | | 1st h. 37 | |

*Chart 14: Tiger Woods*

Sports that take a certain amount of finesse and talent will exemplify the 3<sup>rd</sup> and 5<sup>th</sup> houses. These houses have been seen before for great communication skills and talent. And if the athlete is successful in terms of financial rewards the 2<sup>nd</sup> and the 11<sup>th</sup> houses must come into play. Again with someone with incredible skills and talents we see an extraordinary 3<sup>rd</sup> house. Here is the ruler of both money houses 2 and 11 in the 3<sup>rd</sup> house. This explicitly means the person becomes wealthy through their talents and skills using their hands. The 3$^{rd}$ house rules the hands as in writing and in their use in any creative endeavor. Golf uses the manipulation of the hands like most sports.

Neptune can sometimes mean some kind of special gift from beyond this world. His Mars also aspects this house and it rules the sign Scorpio so it is aspecting a house it rules, meaning it strengthens this house all the more for the attributes this house rules. Additionally, Jupiter aspects this house and the planet's there in, Venus, Moon and Neptune. This house is full of gifts, talents and is fortified to the ultimate, from Mars and Jupiter.

He has Mercury in the 5$^{th}$ house of talent and intelligence. This is the house of the mind and he has to have a very calculating mind to be this successful in such an individualistic sport. Mercury rules his Virgo ascendant. This connects the 1$^{st}$ house with the 5$^{th}$ house. This gives inspiration and luck. Saturn aspects the 5$^{th}$ house by opposition and it is aspecting Mercury, which gives the mind a very deep contemplative focus that one would need to excel in this sport. Saturn is aspecting the sign on the 5$^{th}$ house Capricorn, and it rules Capricorn so it powers up this house all the more with its concentration of mental focus and power.

Notice, when individuals have a chart where the 3$^{rd}$, 7$^{th}$ and 11$^{th}$ houses are aspected by Jupiter, (Jupiter is in one of these houses) the person is successful from all 3 of these houses. The trine aspect of Jupiter connects these houses indicating the individual will be talented and will have opportunities through the empowered 11$^{th}$ house to express the talent and receive rewards. In Tiger's chart Jupiter in his 7$^{th}$ house aspects the 3$^{rd}$ house planets plus Saturn in the 11$^{th}$ house of gains. His destiny was certain with this powerful chart for skills, talent and mental focus.

# The 7th House: Commitment and Sharing Life

*We are never more discontented with others than when we are discontented*
*with ourselves*

*Henri Frederic Amiel 1821-1881*

**Jaya Bhava:** Relationships, marriage, business and business partnerships, contractual agreements, sexual passions, courts, open enemies, divorce, residence in foreign lands, impotency, desire, and kidneys.

**Kendra. Kama.**

## Sharing and Support in Relationships

The 7th house and sign Libra is about the one-on-one relationships, which make up our commitments. It is about learning to share. Most especially, it is about sharing your life with another. Sharing takes a certain amount of compromise and balancing. Relationships give us a sense of wholeness and completion, in the sense that someone understands and supports us. This is a need and desire that validates our feelings. We all have the innate desire to share our life with someone who understands and validates us. Perceiving ourselves through someone else's eyes gives us validation and love, which gives our life meaning.

When we commit to another we are giving of ourselves to the needs and wants of others. To give yourself over to another requires the process of sharing. Sharing means we give our time and energy to others. From this we begin to experience things from another's perspective.

To share is always a good experience because we get to share our ideas, communicate what is on our mind and giving a different perspective through someone else's mind. This gives understanding and caring. We feel more complete when we share an idea or experience. When feeling alone and incomplete sharing an idea gives a feeling of completion in the transaction of information.

## Expectations in a Commitment

The 7th house represents the kind of people we attract in marriage. Marriage is a commitment to another to live the rest of your life together. Many are afraid of making such a lifelong commitment. It all seems so permanent. This can be devastating in many cases with such elaborate ceremonies and the commitments made at the time of a marriage are sealed in an array of expectations. So when these commitments and expectations are not met the marriage goes bad and the relationship begins to unravel.

Anger surfaces when commitments are not kept. Over a long period of time of not doing their part in a relationship many covert and passive aggressive behaviors come out for not carrying out their perceived end of the bargain. These are at the culprit of relationship issues. The process of realizing one cannot continue in a certain relationship can bring many feelings of failure which create deep sadness for many dreams, hopes and expectations formally believed become failures in life.

## Business Partnerships

In business partnerships agreements, expectations and fairness are expected to carry out their end of the bargain. And when expectations are not met the business deal can go sour and is not fruitful or productive. In a business partnership a deal is accepted that both parties will contribute equal shares into the working contract.

All 7th house matters require that equal shares are put in or there are misconceptions of fairness and can ruin the agreement. Many business or personal relationships are destroyed due to the expectations being unmet.

Generally a business deal comes into action when someone needs another party to supply the needs that one does not have and the two complete a whole. In a business transaction the person who can supply the money or funds unites with the one with the experience or talent to complete a business. Or in a love relationship each contribute attributes to complete a life by providing the parts of the self that one lacks and needs to bring a life of fulfillment.

## 5th house is Love 7th house is Marriage

Interestingly the 7$^{th}$ house is looked at as to the house when someone is going to find a partner, but this is not the house to be analyzed for finding a love relationship because one does not usually jump into marriage when finding a partner. The process of love is a 5$^{th}$ house matter.

Then the process of marriage comes later with the 7$^{th}$ house. The 5$^{th}$ house is courtship and engagement as in falling in love. The 7$^{th}$ house indicates when the wedding or marriage occurs, and once in a marriage this is the house to be analyzed.

A strong 7$^{th}$ house can indicate a leader who directs and can delegate proper responsibilities to others. They bring an array of people together and give power and position to others.

## Compromise

The sign Libra is relative to the 7$^{th}$ house and is ruled by Venus. Libra is the sign of balance, fairness and compromise. There are always two sides to a coin meaning there are two sides to any situation viewed through a relationship. Both have valid reasons for how the relationship is working or not working. But it is in the unspoken expectations that cause the undercurrents that can destroy a relationship.

## Love is a Desire with many ways to Connect

As a Kama (air) house of desire, we all have the innate desire to share and communicate our feelings through our speech. Love is expressed through the expression of thoughts and feelings. The way in which we convey our feelings is a part of how we love each other.

The realm of the Internet and previously the telephone people express their feelings and love through these vehicles instead of being physically together. People are finding love on the Internet through dating services, Face book, Skype, and e-mails. This revolution of connecting others is a means of communication in this global world today.

## Open Enemies

The 7th house is the house of the opponent as in a competition of sports or politics. This is your equal in a match to run against one another. It is the house that predicts the outcome of such contests referred to the house of open enemies.

## Power of Attraction

Venus as the ruler of Libra (7th house) is the power of attraction and brings together a union of two individuals. Mars as the ruler of Aries is relative to the 1st house. Venus and Mars represent the male and female energy brought together as the attractive forces in the need to relate and become one.

The 1st house is sunrise in a chart and represents the beginning of life or beginning of each day. Interestingly, the 7th house is the sunset of the day before the beginning of nightfall. This symbolizes that a relationship is when we lose our own identity to become one or merge with another.

## Procreation

The 7th house rules the external sexual and reproductive organs whereas the 8th house rules the internal sexual organs. Venus and Libra are known to be a part of procreation as Venus is Shukra in Vedic astrology actually means semen, which is the source of procreation in a man. And in Greek mythology Aphrodite actually means of the sea foam where she arose out of the castration of Cronus into the sea. Relationships and the sexuality of the sexes coming together are the force that procreates mankind.

## Second Born Child

The 7th house represents the second born child because it is the 3rd house from the 5th house. The sibling (3rd house) to the first-born child (5th House).

## Grandmother

This is the house of the grandmother because it is the 4th house from the 4th house (mother), which is the mother's mother.

## Rules Kidneys

Libra and the 7th house also rule the kidneys, which are the organ that purifies and filters all the liquids in the body.

## Maraka House

The 2nd and 7th houses are the maraka houses. Maraka means "killer. This means these houses have a grave effect on the length of life. This is because the houses of length of life or longevity are the 8th and 3rd houses. It is because both the 2nd and the 7th houses are 12th from the houses of longevity. At the time of death a person will be in a dasha of a planet ruling or in a maraka house, either 2nd or 7th houses, but also there must be associations to the 8th house of death as well.

# Bhavat Bhavam

## The Seventh House

**It is the 1st from the 7th.**

**It is the 7th from the 1st.** The core issue of the 7th house is our **relationships** that are partnerships. Technically these relationships are contractual, figuratively and literally. This includes our marriage partner and our business partnerships. Since it is the house opposite the 1st house, the 7th house is a reflection of us. Because it is the house of business partnerships it is a house that will indicate career and profession in business.

**It is the 4th from the 4th house.** This is the house of our mother's mother or our maternal grandmother. It is where our basic security and protection originate. It is real estate acquired from the mother.

**It is the 10th from the 10th house.** This pertains to our business and our profession as a career, also our career goals, advancements and our reputation. This house indicates how well we will do in business.

**It is the 6th from the 2nd house.** This indicates making money in a service-oriented career such as restaurants or health. The 6th house representing our health and the 2nd house is what we eat indicating the healthiness of our diet.

**It is the 2nd from the 6th house.** This is the house of money from our work efforts. It is also how healthy we eat.

**It is the 5th from the 3rd house.** This refers to our sibling's children (nieces and nephews) especially our youngest sibling. It can also be our ability to communicate.

**It is the 3rd from the 5th house.** This is the house that represents the second born child since it is the 3rd sibling from the 5th the first-born. It is our first child's ability to communicate. It is our ability to communicate and write, particularly contracts. Also it is the learning skills and travels of our children especially the first-born.

**It is the 8th from the 12th house.** This is the house of the end of loneliness or sorrow. It is deep research on dreams or meditation.

**It is the 12th from the 8th house.** This is the end of life, since the 8th house is life and death. This house represents the end of life. It is a maraka house. Maraka means killer. It can reveal how you will die, the causes. It is loss of inheritance and loss or end of obsessions and suffering.

**It is the 11th from the 9th house.** It is the wealth and gains received from the father. It can tell about the father's friends and hopes and dreams. It is our spiritual rewards.

**It is the 9th from the 11th house.** It is spiritual organizations or the beliefs of our friends or groups we are involved in. It may indicate travel with our friends or groups. It is the eldest sibling's spirituality or beliefs.

# Planets in the 7th House

## Sun

The spouse can be controlling and demand to be the center of attention while the partner stands in their shadow. Marriage works when the spouse takes command and charge. The partner can be very successful but egotistical. The material grandmother is very powerful and may play an important role in life. The second born child is confident and secure. As a leader in business affairs great success is granted through the power to delegate others.

## Moon

Partnerships can be unpredictable and change often. The partner can be very changeable and are overly sensitive and hard to read. Depending on the sign the partner could be notable or famous. The material grandmother is nurturing but elusive, meaning hard to connect with, but will have a powerful effect on the life. The second born child is very sensitive and emotional and needs more attention. Business affairs are important and the support of many friends brings opportunities. Recognition or fame comes in the chosen field of work.

## Mercury

Partners are fun and easy to be with because of communication skills, intelligence and sense of humor. Having a sense of humor is a very important requirement in the choice of partners. There is an attraction to someone younger or young at heart. The material grandmother is sharp and intelligent promoting education. The second born is smart witty, and well liked. They should be directed into a field of communications. Business communications are successful and can indicate a spokesperson for a business.

## Venus

Partners are very attractive and attentive in love and romance, and many drawn to them. It is hard to not notice the attention they receive. This can put a damper on relationships. Business relations are good because of new and creative ideas brought to the workplace. The material grandmother is creative, charming and attracts a lot of attention. The second born child is beautiful and creative and should be directed into a field of the arts.

## Mars

This position is hard on relationships, this is called Kuja Dosha. When Mars aspects the 7th house marriage is extremely difficult. The partner will have anger issues, causing them to be combative and difficult maybe even violent. If Mars is weak, in Cancer or with Ketu the partner will not be openly combative but passive aggressive. They can be extremely bright and intelligent. The material grandmother has personal problems negatively affecting the home life. The second born child is ambitious and very athletic. Success in work will create an independently owned business.

## Jupiter

The partner is a powerful leader, or a teacher, but can be overbearing with strong opinions, being a know it all. In a female's chart the spouse is very complex and requires a lot of attention. Great respect comes from being successful and powerful in business. The material grandmother is overbearing and demanding at family occasions. The second born child is very intelligent and wise but prone to weight problems. Children will play an important part in the marriage.

## Saturn

Marriage takes on a serious role in life. The partner can be very powerful but cold, detached or older. Saturn is most powerful in this house (dig bala) so its placement gives marriage longevity. In many cases the marriage is sustained long overdue. The material grandmother is distant or dies early, or is never known. The second born child is very protective and ultra responsible and may be the caretaker of the family. Business partners can be very helpful if put in control.

## Rahu

The partner is powerful and over bearing in many ways. They have an addictive personality, be careful around this issue. Their fun side could turn into a dark and destructive side if not watched. Extreme events will plague the marriage and suspicious tendencies of ulterior motives cause problems. The partner is very successful but obsessive in their work spending very little time home. The material grandmother has a colorful past, which could be very turbulent and destructive, particularly for the mother. The second born child has a life of fate and destiny, which is probably influenced by the powerful father.

## Ketu

The partner is very needy, playing the part of a victim. They may need help, but are reluctant to change and do what is needed. There is an attraction for partners who need help, as an underdog or outcast in society. A sense of power and confidence is achieved with the ability to help. There is always something missing in the area of relationships, never bringing fulfillment always being the giver. The spouse will have very light colored or very different eyes. On rare occasions the partner is very spiritual but their detachment will cause a sense of lack in the relationship. The material grandmother is very detached, or non-existent, but very perceptive. The second born child may have emotional or physical problems maybe due to problems with the father.

# Ruler of the 7<sup>th</sup> House in the

## 7<sup>th</sup> house

The partner is very present and makes a strong impact on the life. They are there when you need them, depending on the sign. Planets in debilitation can represent a weak partner and planet in their own sign may become overbearing.

## 8<sup>th</sup> house

The partner is very secretive and not very trustworthy. This is a very difficult placement for marriage and may indicate divorce. Issues around betrayal cause separation. There is a major lesson to be learned pertaining to trust through relationships.

## 9<sup>th</sup> house

The partner is very philosophical and spiritual but can be a bit overzealous in their opinions. The partner has a love of travel and education indicating many trips together. The partner is met through college, travel, or church.

## 10<sup>th</sup> house

The partner is met through the profession or they work together in business. The partner is very ambitious and successful. The partner's family will be close and play a big role in life, especially the mother-in-law. There may be a family business.

## 11<sup>th</sup> house

Friends or social events arranged through friends bring opportunities that connect you to your partner. It is important to have a partner that has the same passions to help make the world a better place and must be friends as well as lovers.

## 12<sup>th</sup> house

Losses around relationships cause emptiness in the heart. The partner travels extensively indicating loneliness and isolation. The partner may be a foreigner or have many differences.

## 1<sup>st</sup> house

Doing many things together unite and bond the relationship, with great attention, involving all activities. Partnerships of all kinds are important but too much attention could be the loss of the self. Always giving with no receiving can disrupt a relationship.

## 2<sup>nd</sup> house

The partner is very successful financially but places too much emphasis on money matters. They are concerned about how their money is being spent. Their voice is loud and strong especially when expressing their financial concerns.

### 3rd house

The spouse is met through school, college or childhood. It is important to travel together. Marriage will have many ups and downs due to the partner's hard headedness.

### 4th house

The partner is concerned with family life and seeks the security and protection a warm cozy family brings. Family gatherings are a source of pleasure and happiness. The partner directs and controls the family events.

### 5th house

Children play a very important part of the marriage, and keep it together. The partner values the children in a relationship. The spouse can be very loving and playful but can have a wavering mind looking for affairs.

### 6th house

Conflicts and struggles seem to be a part of marriage and relationships. The partner can be very frustrating but does improve over time. It seems they work excessively for very little pay. Their belief is, being successful means no time off work.

***John Lennon*** was the originator of the legendary rock group the Beatles. And as all rock groups go, they must have partnerships to make their career a success. The 7th house as the house of partnerships rules both love and business, John has Sun, Rahu, and Mars in Virgo in the 7th house His partnerships with the other Beatles, Paul, George and Ringo brought great success and they were able to harmonize their voices beautifully.

| 1st h. 32 | 2nd h. 24 | 3rd h. 22 | 4th h. 37 |
|---|---|---|---|
| ASC 26:52 Rev / ℧ 17:59 Rev | ♄℞ 20:11 Bha / ♃℞ 20:39 Bha | ♅℞ 02:31 Kri | |
| | John Lennon | | ♀ 11:09 Pus |
| 10:30 Shr | Wed 10-09-1940 / 18:30:00 / Liverpool / England / Timezone: -1 DST: 0 / Latitude: 53N25'00 / Longitude: 02W55'00 / Ayanamsha : -23:01:50 Lahiri | | ☿ 10:11 Mag |
| 10th h. 29 | ☿ 15:31 Swa | ♆ 02:59 UPh / ♂ 09:37 UPh / ☊ 17:59 Has / ☉ 23:14 Has | |
| | 9th h. 27 | 8th h. 24 | 7th h. 23 |

*Chart 15: John Lennon*

But there was great turmoil and fighting with all of John's partnerships from the other Beatles (business partners) and marriage. Brian Epstein their manager lost a substantial amount of business and money for the Beatles and John's wife Yoko Ono played a big part in the breakup of the Beatles. Incidentally, Rahu in the 7th house can indicate a foreigner for the wife and he had a fascination for foreigners, as Yoko Ono is Japanese.

Mars is combative but ambitious as his partner Paul McCartney was very driven and ambitious. He could not have achieved as much without the driving force of others. It was once noted that Paul was the reason why so many songs were recorded because he made them go to work every day. He is still recording music and traveling with concerts at age 70. Mars rules the 2nd house of money and the 9th house of blessings and luck. So Mars is a great blessing for him in this house even though he fought it all the way. Mars is very bad for relationships in the 7th house. The Sun as the ruler of the 6th house in the 7th that caused a lot of the fighting and disagreements. Rahu in the 7th house is the magnifying force that made their rock group the legendary Icon of the rock and Roll era. Rahu many times represents fame and fortune but with a price to pay.

Mercury is the ruler of the 7<sup>th</sup> house in the 8<sup>th</sup> house indicating turbulence in marriage with divorce. He was married twice and separated once before with Yoko. There was no room for compromise, his demanding partners had to be the center of attention with Sun and Rahu. His Mercury in the 8<sup>th</sup> house caused distrust and problems in all relationships. The 7<sup>th</sup> house is a maraka house meaning "killer", indicating a short-lived life with three malefics Sun, Rahu, and Mars, and additionally the ruler of the 7<sup>th</sup> house goes to the 8<sup>th</sup> house of death. At the time of his death he was in the dasha of Jupiter/Mercury. Mercury rules the 7<sup>th</sup> house, which is a maraka house and resides in the 8<sup>th</sup> house of death and Jupiter is in the 2<sup>nd</sup> house a maraka house and is aspected by Mercury the ruler of the 7<sup>th</sup> house (maraka). Maraka houses and the 8<sup>th</sup> house are indicated at the time of death.

*Jacqueline Kennedy Onassis* was the wife of President John F Kennedy. Her life of fame and fortune was besieged with great pain and suffering. As the wife of President Kennedy she was tormented with his secret affairs with other women. He was secretly involved with Hollywood movie stars such as Marilyn Monroe. After President Kennedy was assassinated she moved to Greece to escape the fear that the forces that killed her husband would take her children. There she married the Greek shipping tycoon Aristotle Onassis. He took her to his privately owned Island of Skorpios where she could feel protected.

*Chart 16: Jacqueline Kennedy*

She has the Moon and Rahu in Aries in the 7<sup>th</sup> house, which together represent famous partners. The Moon indicates the masses or public and Rahu magnifies this energy to the maximum degree. The Moon rules the 10<sup>th</sup> house, which indicates the career, power, fame and social standing. It was her marriage to a President that brought her to the attention of the world and she was the most photographed celebrity of her time. Aristotle Onassis was also very famous and one of the richest men in the world during the time Jacqueline was married to him. Here the extremes in partners are represented by this powerful combination in the 7th house.

Mars rules the 7th house and is in the 11th house of great wealth and great gains. She became exceedingly wealthy through her marriages. Mars is with Neptune indicating the mystery and scandals that surrounds her husbands. The assassination of her husband John F Kennedy has never been resolved and Neptune points to his affairs. Aristotle Onassis also died leaving her a great inheritance but a struggle with his daughter Christina.

# The 11<sup>th</sup> House: Hopes and Dreams

*Hope is the dream of a waking man.*

*Aristotle BC 384-322*

*There is no medicine like hope, no incentive so great, and no tonic so powerful as expectation of something tomorrow.*

*Orison Swett Marden 1850-1924*

**Ayaya Bhava:** Great gains, attainment of desires, gains from profession, wealth, money that comes in large amounts, money from side ventures, friends, groups, organizations, humanitarians, eldest sibling, left ear, ankles.

**Upachaya. Kama.**

## Friendships

The 11th house and sign Aquarius is about our ultimate desires. It involves our hopes and wishes. In terms of our relationships, these are things we usually share with our friends. Friendships put us in touch with community. The 11th house and sign bring out our humanitarianism, and our desire to be in touch with the greater whole of humankind. This includes groups and organizations where people can feel connected and share common interests.

The sense of feeling heard by our friends gives us a feeling of connection and without this feeling we cannot thrive or find our sense of joy and happiness. To share our thoughts and feelings through the communication of our friends gives us a sense of a life well lived. The air triplicity is about sharing our thoughts, feelings, and connecting through others. This is an essential part of being a human being and we could not exist without this connection and the ability to learn cooperation and support for each other. We need each other, to support, love, communicate and exist.

The air element is about desires. These manifest in the form of thinking, relating, and communicating. Gemini is the first air sign; five signs away is Libra, and nine signs away from Gemini is Aquarius. These three signs are called the air triplicity. They deal with ways of communicating our thoughts, and our relationships in life. Houses 3, 7, and 11 relate to air. These are called the kama houses.

## Affluent and Powerful People

The 11th house is the most advanced of the air signs it concerns the highest of values and aspirations. This pertains to our hopes, wishes and desires, which is why this house has the power to grant great gains. The fact that this house is about friends and organizations involving people means our wishes, dreams and gains comes from the involvement with other people. This is the house of powerful and affluent people.

## Aquarius and Humanity

Ouranos (Uranus ruling Aquarius) is the sky god in Greek mythology. The sky god is above the earth portraying the heavenly father who is above to protect, while in Indian Myth Varuna is the sky god and rules the nakshatra **Shatabhishak,** which is in the middle of Aquarius. The Symbol is an empty circle or a thousand flowers or stars. This nakshatra is the large group of faint stars in the Water Bearer. So here is the vision of the 11th house relative to the sign Aquarius.

Whereas the 5th sign Leo relative to the 5th house is about the sole purpose of an individual to express themselves, Aquarius is the 11th sign relative to the 11th house is about people coming together to express themselves as the whole of humanity. ;

In the constellation of Leo there is the one and brightest star visible to us which is Regulus known as the heart of the Lion, but in the constellation of Aquarius it appears as a haze of light which is the combination of many stars shining together representing the many stars of humanity.

## Community, Social Efforts and Oneness

The 11 house represents the power of the many coming together to manifest the power of combining our energies as one to create a world of peace and love. As part of the air triplicity this involves the importance to magnify our feelings expressed through the need to communicate as a community and social effort. This is the magnification of the desire to commune together and that is expressed though the power of the masses uniting. This means we must learn to work together to unite as one. This is the power of oneness and the opening of minds in a way that understands and embraces unity. To unite together and uplift others is a part of the process of the 11th house.

## Power of Hope

Because it is the 2nd house from the 10th house it is the ability to make great gains or wealth through our work, therefore this can be the reason for gains being a part of this house. But the greatest power of this house involves the power of hope, and the aspiration to fulfill our dreams. This great achievement and power cannot be attained without the commitment of others to help us rise to the top of our field and aspirations.

## House of Oldest Sibling

Whereas the 3rd house is the youngest sibling the 11th house is the oldest sibling, as a house of relating, and this indicates the relationship with the eldest sibling. The oldest is the most respected therefore making Saturn the natural ruler of Aquarius the 11th sign and the youngest sibling is relative to Mercury which rules the 3rd sign Gemini. Saturn represents older and Mercury younger.

## Rules the Left Ear

The 3rd house rules hearing, which is no surprise, since most communications come through the process of listening. The air signs are primarily about communications to others through relationships. But the 11th house is the ultimate house of these vast communications skills as in our communities and the global reaches of the masses and the world. Consequently, it specifically pertains to the left ear while the 3rd house is more specific to the right ear. The left ear is more in tune with the more intuitive side of the right brain meaning listening through the ears or humanity. This indicates the broad communications of the masses together and the understanding as one.

## Rules Legs and Ankles

The 11<sup>th</sup> house pertains to the legs and ankles therefore this is the house that can give us balance and stability in a fragile world. The ankles give us stability and the power to move forward. The ankles are the connecters to our feet and are very small in comparison to the weight of the body. This is our connection to the greater whole and that it must pass through the small individual connection of our ankles to ground us from the world above to the grounding world below.

In relation the ankles those with strong planets here are good dancers, and know how to move through the vehicle of the legs and feet.

## Sign of Astrology

"As above so below!" There is a reference in this sign to astrology as to connecting us to the world of the sky and the world of humanity and all beings on this earth.

# Bhavat Bhavam

## The Eleventh House

**It is the 11<sup>th</sup> from the 1<sup>st</sup>.**

**It is the 1<sup>st</sup> from the 11<sup>th</sup>.** The 11<sup>th</sup> house's core issue is **desire**. It is the results of our materialistic desires. It is the house that brings great gains and wealth. This house deals with money that comes in large sums. It multiplies the things represented by the planets placed here. In Vedanta it is believed it is our desires that keep us reincarnating here therefore this house can bring the many problems associated with attachments to the material world. It also rules friends, groups, associations and humanitarian efforts. Our friends are our way of validating ourselves through someone outside ourselves thus gives us a feeling of connection, something we all need. Socializing with others that have the same interest gives us a sense of belonging. This can be a very political house on a higher level being opposite the 5<sup>th</sup> house of politics. It is the organizational ability of groups and people. It rules the eldest sibling as well.

**It is the 12<sup>th</sup> from the 12<sup>th</sup> house.** This is the house of the end of loss and expenditure therefore; it is the house of gains.

**It is the 6<sup>th</sup> from the 6<sup>th</sup> house.** This is another house for health and the healing of disease; generally it is recovery from illness.

**It is the 10ᵗʰ from the 2ⁿᵈ house.** This is the house of fame and wealth. It can indicate a career working with finances or banking.

**It is the 2ⁿᵈ from the 10ᵗʰ house.** This house indicates the wealth and money we acquire from our career.

**It is the 9ᵗʰ from the 3ʳᵈ house.** This is the house of higher learning. It has to do with travel either short or long distances. It indicates publishing our writings. It can indicate our siblings (especially the youngest) relationship with the father.

**It is the 3ʳᵈ from the 9ᵗʰ house.** This is the house of the travels, courage and teaching from the father. It is our father's siblings therefore, our paternal aunts and uncles.

**It is the 8ᵗʰ from the 4ᵗʰ house.** This is a house of the death or disgrace of the mother, therefore is the house to look for in adoption.

**It is the 4ᵗʰ from the 8ᵗʰ house.** This is another indication of adoption since it is the mother that comes from death or separation. Security from abandonment, in other words because of the loss of a mother, another mother (adoptive) will provide security.

**It is the 7ᵗʰ from the 5ᵗʰ house.** This house will indicate our first-born child's spouse. It is business partnerships with our children (especially the oldest).

**It is the 5ᵗʰ from the 7ᵗʰ house.** This can indicate your spouse's children from a previous marriage. It can indicate the mind or advice given by our spouse.

# Planets in the 11ᵗʰ House
## Sun

Humanitarian efforts are very dear to the heart. There is involvement in groups and organizations that create change in the community or the world. As a leader they are asked to head or lead groups and organizations. This may involve local community schools, meetings to direct work, business or political groups. These groups are connected to powerful people in the community. The father is successful, well connected and influential. Friendships are valuable. Friends are powerful leaders mainly males but can be bossy and controlling. Financial gains from work come from the connection to powerful influential people. The oldest child will attract a powerful and controlling partner.

## Moon

Friendships are valuable but are not deep or long term; they may be superficial, with many acquaintances. There is great popularity with all the surrounding people, in childhood to adulthood. But rarely are there deep and lasting friendships. They seek out council and cause emotional drain. The vast majority of friends are female. The oldest child may be undecided about marriage and changes partners often. Helping in many political groups makes one weary with unfinished business. The mother may be disconnected and separated from you at birth.

## Mercury

Communication skills are superior giving opportunities to be assigned as the spokesperson for many groups or organizations. The sense of humor, adaptability and open-mindedness gives popularity and many friends. Money comes from the ability to speak well and appeal to diverse groups. The education is endorsed by many organizations. Recognition comes from the younger generation and the cutting edge of what is new. The oldest child will marry someone intelligent and possibly younger.

## Venus

Success comes easy, with great family connections. The father may be noted in the community and is helpful throughout life. Wealth and money predominate the life with the ease and comfort of great luxuries. Promotion of the arts, creativity and artistic pursuits are a part of the values and the community. Popularity gives the opportunity to represent many organizations. Grace and charm come natural, and social graces are innate. The oldest child will marry a charming attractive partner.

## Mars

Friends may be a problem throughout life, attracting many jealous difficult people always in competition. There is a love of athletic groups or sporting events. Friends may have ulterior motives. Great wealth from the career comes from drive and ambition. The father is a motivating source for career success. The oldest child will have problems in marriage and must marry when older.

## Jupiter

Wisdom and wise council are revered and gain popularity in the community. Many groups, political and social seek advice. Wealth, money and luxuries are bestowed through work and a head start may have come from family. The father achieved financial gains. Influential people are a great benefit throughout life as resources. The oldest child will marry an influential wealthy partner.

## Saturn

Friendships are few because of differences with the desire to avoid superficial friendships. Friends are deep and long lasting, and may be childhood friends. As a loner there is no interest in community affairs. The father has difficulty in work matters with loss of money. The ability to bring great wealth from the career is limited unless Saturn is in Libra, Capricorn or Aquarius. These signs have the ability to bring great wealth from work. The oldest child may have difficulty in marriage, for the partner is not emotionally connected, or they may marry someone older.

## Rahu

Rahu in the 11th house can indicate the oldest one of the siblings. The mother may have been separated from birth. There are many very influential and powerful people in life and give opportunities, all in the asking The father is successful and knows people in power. There are connections to people who are in control and are the movers and shakers in the community. The friends are very materialistic having a good and bad side, careful of involvement in financial dealings with them. The partner may have children from a previous marriage. The marriage of the first-born child may cause problems or move far from home.

## Ketu

Unusual friends and groups stand out as a defining aspect of life. The unique and unconventional types are preferred; underdogs or outcasts in society. Groups that are unusual such as metaphysical or spiritual are a part of life. There is a constant yearning to do something that has deep meaning and can help others. Something is always missing about the need to fulfill life with meaning and purpose. Friends cause a drain emotionally and do not give in return. The oldest child will feel a great loss within marriage and relationships attracting those who are troubled.

* The 11<sup>th</sup> house ruler is always a first class malefic planet and the houses it occupies are troubled in some way. But the 11<sup>th</sup> house ruler going to another upachaya house (3, 6, 10, and 11) gives more power and drive for accomplishment in the house it occupies. Remember planets in the 11<sup>th</sup> house prosper and bring wealth but the ruler of the 11<sup>th</sup> house will always be a malefic planet.

# Ruler of the 11<sup>th</sup> House in the

### 11<sup>th</sup> House

Friends are an important part of life, and can be disappointing. Many times they are not around when in need, and do not follow through on promises. Influential friends offer support but ultimately it is for their ulterior motives.

### 12<sup>th</sup> House

Friends disappoint when they leave or move away, and their commitments fall short of expectations. Charities and humanitarian causes are a part of life and occupy a lot of time, money and effort.

### 1<sup>st</sup> House

Organizations are a major part of your life and take a lot of time. Others take advantage of the generous attitude and commitment of sharing in the community. Sharing the wealth gives many blessings.

### 2<sup>nd</sup> House

This is one of the most powerful connections that give great wealth and money. Financial power multiplies with giving and sharing wealth. Money and wealth can bring an array of unforeseen problems. Influential friends are always there for support.

### 3<sup>rd</sup> House

Involvement with educational groups that spread valuable information gives life purpose and meaning. Friends share interest and love of knowledge. Belief in thyself will master the art of selling.

### 4<sup>th</sup> House

The mother has great difficulty to overcome in life. There were times of stress within the home but striving to make amends heals many problems. There are gains through real estate, possibly from the mother.

## 5<sup>th</sup> House

Humanitarian work is a part of the life's purpose. The children of the world are viewed as thy own. Children's charities or the arts are compelling work. Issues and problems to have children inspire humanitarian efforts.

## 6<sup>th</sup> House

Friends and associations come through work. They are supportive and helpful in times of need. The physical constitution is strong with good recuperative powers. Health is a focus and promotes leadership in organizations that indorse health.

## 7<sup>th</sup> House

Relationships can be very complicated with too many people meddling in the affairs. Partners come through associations with friends. But they can bring trouble when the partner objects to these associations.

## 8<sup>th</sup> House

Friends can be a sore aching spot in life, and can turn when you least expect it. Jealousy may be the he motivation of their underhanded behavior. Loss around friends can involve betrayal or even death.

## 9<sup>th</sup> House

The father can be very complex and troubled through a difficult past. There is a quest for spiritual fulfillment but it seems to always fall short due to an overpowering teacher or guru whose ego spoils the message.

## 10<sup>th</sup> House

Career pursuits take a long and winding journey to find purpose. There must be love and passion about work. A connection to powerful people come through work and career.

# Steve Jobs

| 8th h. | 9th h. | 10th h. | 11th h. |
|---|---|---|---|
| ☽ 14:30 UBh | ♂ 05:51 Ash | ☋ 10:10 Ard  ♃℞ 27:16 Pun | |
| ♓ | ♈ | ♉ | ♊ |

| 7th h. | Steve Jobs | 12th h. |
|---|---|---|
| ☉ 12:30 Sat | Thu 02-24-1955  19:15:00  San Francisco, CA  USA | ☿ 00:53 Pun |
| ♒ | | ♋ |

| 6th h. | Timezone: 8 DST: 0  Latitude: 37N46'30  Longitude: 122W25'06  Ayanamsha : -23:14:08 Lahiri | 1st h. |
|---|---|---|
| ♀℞ 21:07 Shr | | ♃ 02:05 Mag  ASC 29:03 UPh |
| ♑ | | ♌ |

| 5th h. | 4th h. | 3rd h. | 2nd h. |
|---|---|---|---|
| ♀ 27:56 USh  ☊ 10:10 Mul | ♆ 04:48 Cht  ♄ 27:55 Vis | | |
| ♐ | ♏ | ♎ | ♍ |

*Chart 17: Steve Jobs*

Jupiter is in the 11th house of great gains in the sign Gemini, ruled by Mercury. Gemini is about information and intellect. His genius opened the door to the informational age of technological devices used today, for example the iPhone and Apple computers. This connects Mercury to Jupiter. Jupiter aspects both Venus and Saturn by the exact degree, this is quite amazing! The planets that Jupiter aspects gives expansion and wealth. This empowers both Venus and Saturn and the houses they rule and occupy. They both indicate creative gifts, Venus in the 5th house and Saturn in the 3rd house. The qualities of planets in the 11th house are always expanded and for Jobs this happens to be the intellect. When Ketu is with a benefic it expands even more the positive quality of the planet. So Jupiter is magnetized and multiplied with Ketu in the 11th house of prosperity and great wealth through his intellect.

Mercury as the ruler of the 11th house of great gains is extraordinary. Mercury rules both houses pertaining to money and wealth, the 2nd and 11th houses. He was a self made billionaire, and all billionaire's have a strong 2nd and 11th house ruler. but what makes his 11th house ruler stand out is that his Mercury is stationary!

Stationary planets are the most powerful planets in a chart. A stationary planet is rare for there are only a few days that a planet is considered stationary. This occurs when a planet is in the process of either turning retrograde or direct. In this cycle it appears to be standing still and is called stationary. This impacts a planet as a focal point of power. This powerful Mercury gives reason for his intellectual capacity and great financial wealth. The 2nd house is the house of speech and his powerful speech at Stanford University will go down in history. It has been called the "Gettysburg Address" of commencement speeches. When a planet stands still it is making a statement, "pay attention, look at me!"

## 11th house of Adoption

Job's mother was an unwed graduate student who gave him up for adoption. The 11th house is the house that pertains to adoption because it is the 8th house (death) from the 4th house of mother. The house Ketu occupies indicates a vacuum or void, where we never feel complete in our lives. Ketu in this house can indicate adoption.

Loss around issues with the mother is indicated when the Moon is in the 8th house, further indicating an adoption.

*Oprah Winfrey* has the most amazing chart for wealth and fortune! She made her fortune through acting and mass media. Inventing herself through insightful informative talk shows that dominated the networks. Her business sense made her the ultimate success and one of the richest women in the world, with her company Harpo Productions. Oprah made it all on her own with all odds against her, being a black woman from Mississippi without a mother. Oprah is a workaholic, never taking time out to have a family or marriage.

| 4th h. 31 | 5th h. 25 | 6th h. 30 | 7th h. 25 |
|---|---|---|---|
| | | 23:26 Mrg | 27:05 Pun |
| **3rd h. 26** | Oprah Winfrey<br>Fri 01-29-1954<br>04:15:00<br>Kosciusko, Alabama<br>USA | 00:42 Pun | **8th h. 20** |
| **2nd h. 25**<br>25:55 Dha<br>15:45 Shr<br>15:37 Shr<br>00:42 USh | Timezone: 6 DST: 0<br>Latitude: 33N03'27<br>Longitude: 89W35'15<br>Ayanamsha : -23:13:13 Lahiri | 00:55 Mag | **9th h. 29** |
| ASC 03:03 Mul | 00:21 Vis<br>11:10 Anu | 02:50 Cht<br>15:49 Swa | |
| 1st h. 29 | 12th h. 31 | 11th h. 30 | 10th h. 36 |

*Chart 18: Oprah Winfrey*

The ruler of the 2nd house, Saturn is exalted in Libra in the 11th house. The connection of 2nd house to the 11th is the most powerful connection for wealth and money, but additionally this planet Saturn is exalted, which magnifies this all the more.

Furthermore, the ruler of the 11th house is Venus and it is in the 2nd house, another connection of the house of money (2nd house) to the house of great gains (11th house). Actually, this is a really strong connection for both Saturn and Venus are in each other's sign of ruler ship. Venus is in Capricorn ruled by Saturn and Saturn is in Libra ruled by Venus. This is called mutual reception (parivartana yoga) and when this occurs with the 2nd and 11th house rulers you are assured great wealth.

The 2nd house ruler Saturn in the 11th house exalted denotes a great ability to use her voice. She has brought to the forefront many humanitarian issues never talked about. She is a humanitarian to help those without a voice speak out. Her shows have brought to the surface many issues such as sexual abuse, racism, and homosexuality. She has uncovered and healed many issues concerning human rights an 11th house matter.

# Part IV

# Water Triplicity - Moksha Houses

## 4th House, 8th House and 12th House

*Out of compassion I destroy the darkness of their ignorance. From within them I light the lamp of wisdom and dispel all darkness from their lives.*

*Bhagavad Gita c. BC 400-*

### Moksha

The moksha houses are 4, 8 and 12. They relate to the three water signs (water triplicity). The 4th house relates to the first water sign Cancer, the eighth is Scorpio, and the twelfth Pisces. Of all the aims of life, moksha is the ultimate goal. These are the houses that liberate or free the soul of the chains of earthly karma. They deal with the past, emotions and the essence of the soul. The 4th house can indicate the fear of losing our sense of security. The 8th house is the fear of letting go of control. The 12th house represents releasing all our attachments to the world.

The water houses represent our emotional body and how our experiences affect our soul. The soul is our individual essence that we carry with us from lifetime to lifetime and which leads us into the realms of self-discovery. We want to know how to heal the deep emotional scars that plague our lives and imprint our souls. These houses connect us to other dimensions beyond this world.

The 4$^{th}$ house and water sign Cancer is about all those things which give us a sense of security; things that have a feeling of permanence in our life and which we have little control over changing. Our birth family and heritage would seem to be out of our control. Our parents give us our sense of stability, especially the mother. The 4$^{th}$ house symbolizes our need for protection. Protection fulfills our need for security. Our homes are the places where we hope to feel protected and safe. But deep down we know that nothing is permanent, and a deep-rooted fear lurks beneath the surface because of this knowledge. Thus, the water houses are also about our deepest fears. All fear is based ultimately upon fear of the unknown. These houses are concerned with unraveling that which we fear – the unknown.

The 8$^{th}$ house and sign Scorpio is the most misunderstood house of all. It is simply the house of transformation, but the price of such transformation is very difficult for most. It is necessary to undergo a kind of death process in order to transform the self. This means that we need to totally surrender our need to be in control. In effect, this requires the death of the ego. The more one tries to be in control, the more out of control one becomes, and this is manifested in problems such as obsessive-compulsive behavior. The transformation that evolves out of surrender heals the very core of the soul.

The 12$^{th}$ house and sign Pisces is the house of the unconscious. It is the house of release. It is through the release of our secrets and our fears that we free ourselves of physical and emotional pain. Our deepest fear involves the need to be right. This is the house of renunciation. The ultimate healing process that occurs here is the release of resentments. This is the place of forgiveness. This comes with total acceptance of everyone and everything. Here the emotional body is healed, and the soul is cleansed of all the karmas it has accrued in all lifetimes. This is our final liberation. This is moksha.

The natural process of healing occurs in the water houses. They have to do with the past, and with fear-based emotions.

These relate to:

- The fear of threats to our sense of security (4$^{th}$ house),
- Our fear of being out of control (8$^{th}$ house), and
- The fear of releasing all our attachments to this world (12$^{th}$ house).

Of all the aims in life, moksha is our ultimate goal; all the other goals become insignificant by comparison. These are the most important houses of the horoscope, for the transformation of consciousness is the enlightenment of the soul. This is what is meant by our final liberation. We are beyond the chains of karma, and there is no more suffering,

The healing of life's mystery is the process that life takes us through as we experience the moksha houses. First, the 4th house brings us in touch with our soul through feelings of security and protection, and the initial realization (fear) that our life can be threatened. Then the 8th house manifests the sense of being in control, and the realization (fear) that there is no real control. But the 12th house is the ultimate realization (fear) that we must let go of everything and merge with the collective unconscious. As we process these fears it is the ultimate healing. "All is one and one is all." We were never really separate.

All suffering comes from fear. Fear comes from the unknown. The "not knowing" comes from ignorance. Ignorance is what keeps us in the illusion. The truth will set us free.

The moksha houses will give us our connection to God, because when we realize that we cannot control our lives, there is nowhere else to look but within. As we revert to, "may thy will be my will," our peace and connection and wholeness returns.

The water or moksha houses (4, 8 and 12) deal with fear because these houses are where we lose our sense of control. In these houses of mystery we connect to the essence of God through surrender to a higher force. And in some way all three of these houses deal with surrender, which can be death.

## Water Signs and Houses

The water element is about our soul essence. These are the most misunderstood signs and houses. They deal with the ultimate healing of our human condition, and connect us to other dimensions beyond this world. The first water sign is Cancer. This is the fourth sign of the natural zodiac and therefore relates to the 4th house. Five signs from Cancer is the water sign Scorpio, which constitutes the eighth sign or 8th house, and 9th houses from Cancer is the last sign of the zodiac, Pisces. Pisces is the twelfth sign and relates to the 12th house. This is the water triplicity. Houses 4, 8, and 12 relate to water. They deal with emotions, which, when healed, result in our final liberation, freedom of the earthly plane. These houses are called the moksha houses.

All suffering comes from fear. Fear comes from the unknown. The "not knowing" comes from ignorance. Ignorance is what keeps us in the illusion. The truth will set us free. Let us look into the dynamics of the zodiac to help heal our illusions about ourselves. Through this we can find our final liberation. Through the self, all things will be known. This is what is referred to as self-realization.

The water triangle represents our emotional body and how our experiences affect our soul. The soul is our individual essence that we carry with us from lifetime to lifetime and which leads us into the realms of self-discovery. We want to know how to heal the deep emotional scars that plague our lives and imprint our soul

# The 4ᵗʰ House:  Happiness and Security

*The best and most beautiful things in the world cannot be seen or even touched. They must be felt with the heart.*

*Helen Keller 1880-1968*

**Sukha Bhava**: All fixed assets, real estate, home, land and farming, cars, vehicles, masters degrees or doctorates, the masses, state of mind, happiness, passions, emotions, matters of the heart, security, fear of security being threatened, things that are permanent or lasting forever, the soul, endings, past, conditions at the end of life, heredity and genes, mother, breast, physical heart.

**Kendra. Moksha.**

## Angle, Cardinal and Kendra

The kendra houses are the angles of the chart. These houses are 1, 4, 7 and 10 and are considered the most powerful houses of all. They create the most change and action in a chart. They relate to the qualities of the cardinal signs: 1 - Aries, 4 - Cancer, 7 - Libra, and 10 - Capricorn. These are the houses that bring results. These cardinal signs actually relate to the times of change on earth, which are the times of the equinoxes and change of seasons. The spring equinox (Aries), Summer solstice (Cancer), Fall equinox (Libra), and the Winter solstice (Capricorn). Equinox, both Spring (March 21ˢᵗ) and Fall (September 21ˢᵗ), is when the day and night are equal in duration, and the Winter solstice (December 21ˢᵗ) is the shortest day and Summer solstice is the longest day (June 21ˢᵗ). So these are the power houses in our charts and result in strong action; 1, 4, 7 and 10.

## Happiness and Life Experiences

The 4$^{th}$ house is one of the moksha houses, meaning spiritual liberation. The water houses 4, 8 and 12 are the most misunderstood houses of a chart because they rule the mysteries of life. On the surface the 4$^{th}$ house is known to signify home, security and mother. But there is a much deeper level to this powerful house. This is the house of "Happiness" which is actually based on our past and the deeper essence of security. It is essentially the house of the soul and the end of life.

The 4$^{th}$ house is a house of power and spiritual liberation. It is no wonder it is the house of Happiness.

## Midnight of the Chart

The 4$^{th}$ house is the midnight of the chart. If you are born at midnight your Sun is in the 4$^{th}$ house. Where the Sun is determines the time of day, morning, noon and night. This is midnight where we rebuild through sleep and retreat from the world. This is symbolic of the mystery and profound information that can be understood through this house. In the darkness and time spent away from the world transformation occurs.

## Heredity

In understanding heredity and the 4$^{th}$ house it can followed around the chart in terms of the 4$^{th}$ house from the 4$^{th}$ house is the 7$^{th}$ house, which is our mother's mother (grandmother), the 4$^{th}$ house from the 7$^{th}$ is the 10$^{th}$, our great grandmother, and the 4$^{th}$ house from the 10$^{th}$ is the 1$^{st}$ house, out great, great grandmother, and the return to our own actual 4$^{th}$ house would be the 4$^{th}$ from the 1$^{st}$ house which is our great, great, great grandmother in which makes sense that this distant relative is most like ourselves. So this relates to the family heritage and past by looking through the 4$^{th}$ house.

The house the Moon resides in a chart will be the area of the most change and fluctuation in life.

## Rules the Stomach, Breast and Heart

Feelings are the core of who we are and what we become, even our illnesses are both genetically inherited disease and our feelings, which manifest disease. But could it be we inherit our diseases by means of inheriting the social upbringing in a family? If so, this is a 4$^{th}$ house matter.

The 4th house and the Moon represent the stomach, and the feeling of fullness. A full stomach can feel very comforting, nurturing and satisfying. This gives a temporary feeling of security.

Food and mothers provide nourishment, as the breasts are a means of nourishment for babies. Cancer of the breast occurs in families and is seen as a genetic disease. But could the 4th house in terms of inherited genes that cause disease also indicate inherited temperaments due to culture, upbringing or social conditions?

The Moon is the receiver of the Sun's light and reflects the light back to earth. The 4th house pertains to the Heart as in receiving love or feeling loved. The 5th house also rules the heart but is about giving love. The 5th house is about expression and creativity. The Sun rules the 5th sign Leo relative to the 5th house. The Sun is the giver of life and is the ability to give and express love. (The fixed star Regulus is in the constellation of Leo and is the star of the "heart of the Lion" which depicts the heart energy of the sign Leo).

Heart disease occurs when blood flow is constricted. A broken heart can actually have the effects of physical aching in the heart. When someone dies of a heart attack associated to loss of love it usually pertains to the 4th house for they feel unloved and rejected.

The Moon is a reflection of the past and Cancer is the sign most associated with the past. The 4th house, Moon and Cancer are indicators of the past and sometimes too much energy here can cause people to be stuck in the past. And when stuck in the past you don't allow yourself to have a future. Looking in the rear view mirror will only result in a wreck, or wrecked life. Not being able to process past events and move on creates resentments, which prevent growth and healing. Could this attachment to the past and resentments be a factor in the disease of cancer? And is this maybe where the disease got its name?

## Emotions and Conditioning

The 4th house is about our mind in terms of emotional conditioning. Emotional conditioning determines our outlook on life and will ultimately determine the result of our life.

The Moon is the planet that rules the sign Cancer, therefore contributes to the meanings and experiences of the 4th house. The Moon rules our mind called "manas," which is controlled through our emotional body or feelings. The mind and the emotions are tied together and produce our reactions and impulses to responses in life. It is in the 4th house that our mind is conditioned through our family, upbringing, culture and society. Here is where our beliefs are formed. They are ingrained at an early age and produce our reactions to life experiences. Genetically, we are born with certain abilities and attributes, which come from the 4th house. Can we take charge of our lives through mastering the mind suppressing the control of our emotions and feelings? This again is a 4th house matter.

The way we view our world will result in our sense of happiness. If you are taught to fear or be angry at the world you will experience these emotions. Cultures and our heritage imprints on our soul too. American Indians, Afro Americans and Aborigines carry emotional scars from their ancestry. This is much like the many who are uprooted from their homes (4th house). It is when the home is disturbed that the sense of security is threatened and the foundation of life destroyed. Without a foundation a home cannot be built. Whether it is in the genes or upbringing (probably both), it affects the outlook on the world. This involves the 4th house which is the core and root of our soul. The family, mother or place of birth cannot be changed, it is a permanent condition. Our past is unchangeable.

## End of Life and "Going Home"

The 4th house as the end of life, calls back our soul essence to return home to the source. Going home is the sense of going back to where you came from. There is no better feeling than going to the place where you feel nothing but love. Many have tried to express this feeling of unconditional love, devoid of judgment or condemnation, when they have a near death experience (NDEs). They describe a brilliant white light of love, indescribable in human words. This feeling is total and complete HAPPINESS.

In all of life we have the urge to return home. To return home is likened to merge with God to return to the eternal home which is where we merge with the unconditional, timeless, connection to all or oneness. The sense of being is wholeness and completion, no more separation.

## Movies

Many movies give a deeper meaning to the words "home." Throughout the movie *ET*, the alien asks only to return HOME. In the movie *Powder*, his request is always to go home, which is a basement hidden away from the ignorance of the world. In which ultimately he finally returns to the eternal home when he merges with the energy of God. And in the *Wizard of Oz* Dorothy's only request is to go home, saying, "There's no place like home." Her illusion or dream was much like life, where we are searching for that which we already have. When she awakens, she realizes the same people are surrounding her as in her dream state and that she has come home. We all have our home right now this very moment and it is within our hearts. Here is where we find our connection and love, and this completes our journey to ourselves. We are the Divine love and happiness we are seeking. This is the 4th house!

# Bhavat Bhavam

## The Fourth House

**It is the 4th from the 1st.**

**It is the 1st from the 4th.** The core issue of the 4th house is **security.** Without a sense of security we are extremely troubled and full of fear. The temporal things of this world that give a sense of security are the things ruled by the 4th house. The 4th house is the mother and the security her nurturing provide. It is our home and real estate or any fixed assets such as any vehicles, cars, boats or airplanes. It is happiness which I believe comes from a deep soul felt sense of security. Without security you feel like any minute the carpet could be ripped out from under you. Unfortunately we will always feel insecure about our existence, for nothing here lasts forever therefore, this realization creates an innate fear. This is the house of end of life. It is also said to rule the degrees we attain such as masters and doctorates. I believe because it provides the opportunity to achieve these, probably from the support or financial backing of our parents. It is also the house of the heart, physically as well as figuratively.

**It is the 12th from the 5th house.** This is endings for children, or the loss of children. This is the loss of love or heartache. It is the spiritual release beyond our spiritual practices.

**It is the 5th from the 12th house**. This is spiritual knowledge from dreams and the intelligence we carry from our past lives. It is the ability to love and forgive children or forgive and let go of the issues from our childhood. It may indicate charity given to children in need. It can indicate secret loves, lovers from the past or an old lover's return.

**It is the 11th from the 6th house.** The results from health regimes such as diet and exercise therefore; it is about healing. It represents the friends we acquire from the work place. It can be gains from hard work or the service industry, what we gain from helping others.

**It is the 6th from the 11th house**. This is service for humanity, the work we do with our friends or health activities with them.

**It is the 10th from the 7th house.** It is the career of our spouse and their social standing, or how the public perceives them. It will determine how we operate in a business partnership.

**It is the 7th from the 10th house.** This rules the outcome of business partnerships, relationships of all kinds formed from your career.

**It is the 9th from the 8th house**. It is the spiritual realizations from change, death or metaphysics. It reveals the good that comes out of difficulty and wisdom that comes from deep research.

**It is the 8th from the 9th house.** It is transformation from our spiritual pursuits. It is the death of the father, therefore; the inheritance we receive from him. It can be disgrace associated with the father. It means change or the death of our beliefs.

**It is the 3rd from the 2nd house.** It is the will to acquire wealth and the ability to make money through communications. It may have to do with sales, writing, artistic ability or travel.

**It is the 2nd from the 3rd house.** This is wealth or income acquired from writing, the arts or travel. It is the wealth or earning ability of our siblings particularly the youngest one.

# Planets in the 4<sup>th</sup> house

## Sun

The mother is strong and overbearing, and makes the decisions for the family. The sense of security may be threatened by dominating people. There is no control in matters close to the heart, maybe because important decisions were always made for them taking away the sense of freedom. Even the residence is decided. The family changes residence to find a better home and security. The home is a place of security and going away for long trips is avoided.

## Moon

The mother is nurturing and gives you a sense of security but there were many changes and disruptions from the family early in life. They feel emotionally connected to the home and family and feel very sentimental and proud of their heritage. Always seeking a way to feel security but cannot seem to feel at home because they try to replicate the past home life that is gone. Security is based on feelings and emotions, which are always fleeting. Frequent changes in residence cause a lack of security and unsettled feelings.

## Mercury

The mother insists on a good education and the best of schools, and inspired learning in the home. The parents were travelers and brought home lessons on culture and the world. With a lot of uncertainty in the home, the family may have been uprooted many times to find a better way of life. The mother is progressive, youthful and educated.

## Venus

The home is pleasing and beautiful, because the mother promoted the arts and instilled an appreciation of beauty and art. The home décor is very beautiful with many works or art. The mother is graceful, charming and beautiful. There was a peaceful happy home life that produced a basic sense of security that carries throughout the life. The luxury of a home and property will come easily.

## Mars

Security and peace of mind are a fleeting idea, for the early home life was full of despair. Arguments and fighting were constant and upsetting with the problems around the mother and siblings. The early environment instilled a lifelong lack of security and peace of mind, with an underlying sense that everything could be lost tomorrow. There is the acquisition of good real estate but it creates big hassles around the upkeep.

## Jupiter

A spacious home or a lot of land surrounds is a essential. A happy home life gives a sense of freedom. Family and friends gather at the house because it is a happy meeting place. Real estate is a good investment and they own valuable property. The mother is nurturing and protective. But if Jupiter is too strong in Cancer, Sagittarius or Pisces the mother may be excessive and cause great emotional problems.

## Saturn

The family is very cold and detached because the mother did not give the love and attention the family needed. There were many rules and regulations in childhood. There is an emptiness felt in the home and a loss around security throughout life. The ability to buy or acquire a home may be too hard to achieve. The mother may be ill or die early. Land may be inherited but brings many problems.

## Rahu

Intense problems around the home and the mother drive them out of the house at an early age. Usually the personality of the mother causes fighting and emotional upsets. Separation is felt throughout life with the mother and an emotional healing never occurs even with constant effort. Security is a means to an end and the entire. Money, love, popularity will be abundant but the sense of security is still scarce.

## Ketu

There is always a sense of loss around the home, family and mother. They are constantly seeking a sense of security through home and family but never feel complete in this area. There seems to be a deep aching and yearning in the heart for a happy home life, and the mother they never had. There is never a sense security within the home. Like a gypsy there is always an unnerving feeling to move, changing residence throughout life.

# Ruler of the 4<sup>th</sup> House in the

## 4<sup>th</sup> House

There is a love of the home and time spent at home. Security and happiness and a desire to own a home is most important. Residence is close to the family and birthplace.

## 5<sup>th</sup> House

The mother provided well and acquired wealth. There is a close residence to the mother and the children are close to the grandmother. Real estate and property may come from family specifically the mother's side.

## 6<sup>th</sup> House

The mother may have many illnesses or need emotional council. The home and family seem to struggle and have debts. The mother worked hard to make ends meet. Aunts and uncles of your mother's side cause the family many problems.

## 7<sup>th</sup> House

The material grandmother played an important role in the upbringing. The mother had to depend on her for many reasons. Work is with your mother and she can be instrumental in introducing the spouse.

## 8<sup>th</sup> House

The mother had a very difficult life and her pain influenced the manner in how she raised the family. There was great difficulty in family life with the loss of many family members. The mother may die early in life. Security is very hard to achieve.

## 9<sup>th</sup> House

The mother is a very wise and spiritual person, maybe a teacher or guide. Lessons around spirituality and truth were always spoken and taught in the home. The mother and father are close and bring togetherness and a tight family.

## 10<sup>th</sup> House

The mother is an entrepreneur or worked to provide a good family life. The parents were successful and had a powerful presence in the community. The father is the controlling force in the family. There is success in a business with real estate.

## 11th House

The mother may be separated at birth for this is the house of adoption being the 8th from the 4th house. The mother may be sickly or have emotional problems. Security is hard to come by for family problems early in life cause emptiness in the heart.

## 12th House

There is great loss for the mother for she may have to move far from home or leave everything behind. This is an indication of living in a foreign country at some time in life or permanently.

## 1st House

There is a great sense security and confidence providing many successes throughout life.. The family instilled great values and respect in the upbringing. Pride of heredity and family gives a good home and happiness.

## 2nd House

The acquisition of great real estate could indicate a career through property and homes. The mother inspired your love of money, which could have a damaging effect on you personally.

## 3rd House

The family life and upbringing was contentious, many fights and arguments with siblings. The mother was in constant turmoil with your siblings. Travel and culture was inherent and taught early. The family was forced to travel and the home was uprooted often with many changes with school.

*Elvis Presley* was one of the original rock and roll artist creating a big controversy and revolution in our culture. The innovator that defies all odds and goes against the status flow with rebellion and genius are the leaders of new trends or revolutions in society. Elvis was magnetic and the heart throb of the 1950s and early 1960s.

| 5th h. 23 | | 6th h. 32 | | 7th h. 28 | | 6th h. 25 | |
|---|---|---|---|---|---|---|---|
| | ♓ | | ♈ ♅ 04:32 Ash | | ♉ | | ♊ |
| 4th h. 27 ☽ 09:04 Sat ♄ 02:47 Dha | ♒ | Elvis Presley Tue 01-08-1935 04:35:00 Tupelo, MS,Mississippi USA Timezone: 6 DST: 0 Latitude: 34N16'00 Longitude: 88W43'00 Ayanamsha : -22:57:14 Lahiri | | | | ♀℞ 02:10 Pun ☊ 08:10 Pus | ♋ 9th h. 30 |
| 3rd h. 18 ☊ 08:10 USh ☿ 06:24 USh | ♑ | | | | | ♃℞ 21:29 PPh | ♌ 10th h. 31 |
| ♃ 29:21 USh ☉ 24:16 PSh | ♐ | ASC 19:23 Jye | ♍ | ♃ 25:06 Vis | ♎ | ♂ 19:52 Has | ♍ |
| 2nd h. 30 | | 1st h. 27 | | 12th h. 31 | | 11th h. 35 | |

*Chart 19: Elvis Presley*

He has a very interesting 4th house for he was a mama's boy and bought his mother lavish gifts such as Cadillac cars and a new house. He has the Moon and Saturn in Aquarius in the 4th house, the house of security, home and mother. It is very interesting to note that many very public and famous people have a powerful 4th house. Specifically the Moon in the 4th house denotes fame, as it aspects fully the 10th house. A good base and solid home is a necessary ingredient for success in the world.

Saturn as the ruler of the 4th house in the 4th house gives a firm and disciplined mother with a detached emotional way of nurturing. Elvis tried to buy security and care for his mother, who had emotional problems. The Moon indicates emotional mood swings and conjunct Saturn will cause depression.

Saturn in Aquarius in the 4th house is Shasha yoga, when Saturn is in the sign it rules in an angular house. This gives a great amount of control and discipline. It can indicate an obsessively controlling nature.

Additionally, Saturn rules the 3rd house, of siblings. He was the survivor of twins, his brother died during birth. So this is at the core of Elvis' issue with his mother. The Moon rules the 9th house, and is with Saturn ruler of the 4th house unites the rulers of an angular and trikona house (Raja Yoga), which brings luck and blessings for the mother. The death of the twin is indicated by the 3rd house, where Venus sits as ruler of the 12<sup>th</sup> house of loss magnified with Rahu.

All of his relationships were tainted by the unhealthy relationship with his mother. She had a very controlling force over him.

**Prince Charles** of Whales is the eldest child to Queen Elizabeth II. He is the oldest heir to the Throne since 1714. Since his mother is the Queen of England he must have a very powerful 4th house. In his 4th house he has Sun, Mercury, and Ketu. The Sun is the ruler of the 2nd house indicating wealth and money from his mother. Mercury as the ruler of the 3rd and 12th house indicates high level of learning and education come from the home and upbringing. The 12th house represents foreign affairs and a job of humanitarian efforts.

| 9th h. 25 | 10th h. 26 | 11th h. 33 | 12th h. 29 |
|---|---|---|---|
| ♓ | ☽ 07:17 Ash<br>☊ 11:49 Ash | ♈ | ♉ ♅ ℞ 06:47 Ard |
| 8th h. 29 | Prince of Engl Charles<br>Sun 11-14-1948<br>21:14:00<br>London<br>England | ASC 12:14 Pus<br>♀ 23:25 Asl | 1st h. 32 |
| 7th h. 20 | Timezone: 0 DST: 0<br>Latitude: 51N30'00<br>Longitude: 00W10'00<br>Ayanamsha: -23:08:24 Lahiri | ♄ 12:07 Mag | 2nd h. 33 ♊ |
| ♐ ♃ 06:44 Mul | ♑ ♂ 27:48 Jye | ♏ ☋ 11:49 Swa<br>☿ 13:49 Swa<br>☉ 29:16 Vis | ♎ ♆ 20:59 Has<br>♀ 23:14 Has |
| 6th h. 30 | 5th h. 23 | 4th h. 29 | 3rd h. 30 |

*Chart 20: Prince Charles*

Ketu shifts the energy of the 4th house to Rahu in the 10th house, the nodal axis, Rahu and Ketu in the 10th and 4th house indicate a famous mother, especially since the Moon is conjunct Rahu in the 10th house.

It is important to know the opposing houses are always affected. The Moon in the 10th house is the ruler of Charles' ascendant; therefore his mother is the ruling force of his life. The 10th house and the Moon indicate the public or masses and he is famous and publically known because of his mother.

# The 8ᵗʰ House: Surrender and Transformation

*Knowledge is power.* \

*Francis Bacon 1561-16*

**Mrityu Bhava:** Death, transformations, change, surrender, control and manipulation, power struggles, mafia, underworld, dark side, secrets, investigation and private investigators, getting to the bottom of things, uncovering the truth, research, study of metaphysics, obsessions, disgrace, scandals, bankruptcy, obstacles, misfortunes, accidents, surgery, length of life, inheritances or money from others such as wills, insurance policies or tax returns, monetary gains from partner, spiritual practices, mediums, intuition, psychic abilities, chronic and long-term sickness, sexual diseases, reproductive organs, elimination organs, life force.

**Dusthana. Moksha.**

## The House of Transformation

The 8ᵗʰ house (and sign Scorpio) is the most misunderstood house of all. It is simply the house of transformation, but the price of such transformation is very difficult for most. It is necessary to undergo a kind of death process in order to transform the self. This means that we need to totally surrender our need to be in control. In effect, this requires the death of the ego. The more one tries to be in control, the more out of control one becomes, and this is manifested in problems such as obsessive-compulsive behavior. The transformation that evolves out of surrender heals the very core of the soul.

The 8$^{th}$ house pertains to control and power. The ways we feel a sense of control and power comes from three areas. They are the most taboo conversational topics: money, sex and death. It is uncomfortable to discuss these subjects, for they are a part of the secretive side. On a personal note you would not normally discuss your bank account, sexual experiences, or death. These issues create great fear in our society because they are part of the unknown. We are lead to believe that money and sex prevents one from attaining spiritual enlightenment. The fear of death controls how we live our life.

## Dusthana and Moksha House

The 8$^{th}$ house is a Dusthana and a Moksha house. Dusthana houses (6, 8 and 12) are the most difficult pertaining to difficulties due to loss, disease, death and sorrow. Moksha houses (4, 8, and 12) are the houses that liberate the soul from the limitations and confines of physical life. They deal with the past, fear-based emotions, and the ultimate process of spiritual realization that comes when we release the past and fear. The suffering experienced from these houses inspires the desire for spiritual liberation.

## Differences between the 8$^{th}$ and 12$^{th}$ houses and Disgrace

The 8$^{th}$ and 12$^{th}$ houses are both dusthana and moksha houses meaning through loss we seek our spirituality. While the 8$^{th}$ house is known as the house of death, the 12$^{th}$ house is the house of loss. Death is a loss and loss is a death. And many times it is hard to differentiate these two houses in terms of experience. The defining difference between these two houses is that the 8$^{th}$ house is about disgrace. The 12$^{th}$ house pertains to loss one feels with endings and letting go, like in the cyclic process of death after a long illness, old age or retirement. Whereas, the 8$^{th}$ house endings are intense and deal with difficult circumstances like divorce, accidents, being fired from a job or murder. The 8$^{th}$ house can be more sudden or forced loss, not letting go as in a cyclic process. So both houses deal with endings, loss and death.

Disgrace is an intense feeling of shame, and embarrassment. Disgrace, shame and embarrassment are all emotions that completely destroy self-esteem or self worth, leading to death unless intervention occurs. This self-loathing initially causes one to fight back through gaining a sense of power over others and the situation. Left unattended extreme ways develop to feel control such as bulling, stealing, sexual abuse, eating disorders, murder or suicide. These negative attempts to get back a sense of control destroy lives. Once outer means of control are exhausted any means of escape are sought to alleviate the inner turmoil and suffering. Escape is sought through addictions with alcohol, drugs, gambling, shopping, or stealing. These are attempts to temporarily feel good about oneself. There seems to be a self-centered all consuming focus with complete exclusion of others. What is obvious to others is initially denied by the addict. Denial is always the beginning stage of transformation and acceptance or surrender is always the final.

## Addictions

The cyclic pattern of addiction is hard to break, and becomes habitual. These feelings are set at an early stage in life and with continual denial and suppression they grow into bigger and bigger problems. The pain of guilt will always surface the truth. Once the truth is brought to light, the shadows will disappear.

This is the meaning of the Greek myth about Hercules and the Hydra. Hercules the strongest man in the world was sought to kill the most horrifying monster the Hydra. This monster had many terrifying swaying heads. As Hercules swung his sword, he cut off the heads and many more grew back immediately. But it wasn't till Hercules got on his knees and brought the Hydra to the light that its dissolved and disappeared. This symbolizes that when we deny our fears and fight back with ego then our fears multiply becoming overwhelming. But when we surrender and bring our fears to the light they aren't so terrifying, they dissolve and disappear. In the light our fears cannot control us, we are released from guilt and shame. There is no longer anything to hide or suppress, the truth will set us free.

## Past and Heritage, Pride or Shame

The moksha houses pertain to the past on a deep level. We all have a sense of who we are based on our past and heritage. Our sense of pride as to what we are is at stake in terms of our self worth. This goes back to our family heritage and experiences around these issues as we develop from an early age. We tend to gravitate to familiar feelings and recreate the experiences we felt in childhood. This motivational factor of familiarity may choose abandonment, loss, poverty or humiliation because it is better than unknown.

Whereas the 4th house pertains to our heritage and gene pool, it also represents our sense of pride in our past based on our family, culture and country. The 8th house takes this to another level of either shame or pride of our past. These appear to be areas we cannot control or change. We cannot change our parents or culture, but without a sense of pride we tend to deny with shame associated to our heritage. When we unconsciously deny a part of ourselves we have no power to change. We direct our focus into areas that distract us from the issue pending. We must be who and what we were born to be or we will be unhappy. We cannot pretend to be something we are not, this is living a lie. We seek validation outside of our selves when we are unsure of ourselves. When we live our lives based on pride and recognition of who we really are, we live a life of fulfillment.

## Near Death Experiences

The near death experience is the ultimate experience that frees the soul to live a life without fear. There is a realization that we never really die. Anyone who has had a near death experience changes with a renewed sense of purpose and passion.

In the book *"Dying to be Me"* by Anita Moorjani has a near death experience (NDE) and came back to tell her story. Her message is simple; we are here to be ourselves. She was dying to be her true self.

## Psychoanalysis

All emotions felt in this psychological place bring us to the core essence and understanding of human nature. The 8th house is the house of psychoanalysis, the introspection of our behavior based on conditions within our environment. But the environment is not everything. Once we uncover the root cause of our emotional reactions, an understanding enables a release of the control it holds on us. Out of the moksha houses comes compassion and understanding, for this is where we are face our greatest fears. These fears are essentially the fear of the unknown. But by understanding the self we understand the unknown. We must face our fears to discover the truth.

## Scientific Research

We innately know the truth of cause and effect. Nature is a force that cannot be denied and reacts through these simple laws. This law or science governs the matter of the physical Universe. When we go against natural laws, imbalance and dysfunction are always the result. Lack of understanding of these fundamental laws causes problems. People confuse the truth of right and wrong with their upbringing of religious dogma but we all innately know the truth. This must be why the 8th house has to do with scientific research, discovering answers to our existence. This is the house of the deepest understanding of causal laws. Great scientist such Einstein have profound planets in the 8th house.

## Metaphysical Sciences

The 8th house is the house of metaphysical studies. Metaphysical means: beyond the physical. These are the sciences that involve forces not capable of being measured by physical means. Love is metaphysical and definitely has a physiological response on the body. Miraculous powers manifest through this house. Metaphysical sciences such as psychology, astrology, or numerology give reason and rational for reasons *"why"* and understanding of the self. These are different from the spiritual studies that are based on faith and trust. Faith and trust comes from the 9th and 12th houses both ruled by Jupiter, the ruler of the 9th and 12th signs, Sagittarius and Pisces. These houses rule spiritual beliefs.

## Mediums, Psychics and Spirit Possession

The 8th house is the house of mediums, channels, intuition and psychic abilities. This is the house connected to other dimensions and to those who have crossed over, it is the house of death. It is the ability to receive messages and guidance from the spirit world, but at times it may involve the dark side of the spirit world, which can involve possession or negative spirit attachments.

Many psychics become private investigators to find missing people. The 8th house is investigation, research and psychic ability. It is the house of metaphysical powers to find the hidden or lost.

## Knowledge is Power

To connect to other worlds and see beyond involves a power that goes outside the understanding of this world. Power is simply knowledge and cannot be abused or it becomes very destructive. Adolph Hitler was known to seek the powers of the occult (hidden sciences) for self gain. He wanted to rule the world. Knowledge is meant to heal the human condition not inflate the ego. When we feel we are separate and overpower others we isolate and destroy ourselves. The 8th house is knowledge that gives power.

## Mars and the Solar Plexus

Mars as the ruler of Scorpio rules the Solar plexus the energy center of our body (Chakra). The solar plexus is about our self-esteem and sense of power. When we are imbalanced in this area we are prone to anger. Mars is the planet of power, energy, drive, ambition, competition, anger and war. When provoked to anger we tend to accuse others, this is a very uncomfortable emotion. Anger lashes out impulsively and is usually based on an unconscious reaction from feelings of injustice we assumed from our past. Analyzing and understanding where these feelings originate heal the response to the stimulus. Growth comes from not casting blame and owning the feeling and consequences. To admit you are wrong is to surrender your false sense of power and gives the opportunity for change.

## Power Struggles, Manipulation, and Empowerment

The 8th house deals with manipulation and power struggles from the dark side. The meaning of a planet comes to govern the world when discovered. Pluto was discovered 1930 when the world was in a very dark place. Mafias were in power and dictators like Hitler began to dominate the world. Pluto brought to the forefront the mythology of Pluto: control, power, the underworld, and secrets. Pluto is associated with the 8th sign Scorpio and the 8th house. During this time the atomic bomb was created indicating the powerful destructive force ruled by this planet, sign and house.

But these forces of nature can be used in a positive way for the secrets of the 8th house can be used to understand and heal. Unfortunately, they were used for self-gain and caused enormous destruction. Manipulating the forces of power out of fear will always destroy, but used in the light of truth and wisdom can unleash the greatest power of the Universe. When we surrender to the higher power our fears dissolve, and the realization we are not in control cultivates the ultimate sense of power through empowerment. The most powerful sense we can attain is through empowerment of others.

## Magnetism and Charisma

An attribute of the 8th house is magnetism and charisma. These are energetic properties someone has that cannot be described, only sensed. Sometimes charisma is used in a way to attract others through seduction and sexuality.

This is the house of sexual obsessions or sexual abuse, and relates to shame indicated by the past and family. Imbalances in this area are usually seen from an early age.

## Controversy, Scandals and Misfortune

The 8$^{th}$ house is a place of difficulty and planets placed here struggle in some way. Since it is the house of life and death our natural instinct is to hold on to life but to cross to the other side we must let go of the natural urge to survive. This is the house of controversy for we are to deny our instincts and urges in order to come to the next level of transition. It is a place of breakthroughs in consciousness and awareness through resistance. It is not natural to dive into the unknown. It can indicate suicide, for this is a jump into the unknown, death.

## Length of Life

The 8$^{th}$ and 3$^{rd}$ house determines the length of life. The 3$^{rd}$ house is our life force and the 8$^{th}$ is how long we live.

In Vedic astrology *"Balarita Yoga"* is when the Moon is in a Dusthana house. It is believed that the Moon in houses 6, 8 or 12 can indicate a short life; a child would not live beyond 12 years old. This of course has to be in combination with other difficulties in a chart, but no doubt this further confirms the 8$^{th}$ house is not about ease and comfort. We are always reminded that this is the house of death.

## Sexual Scandals

The 8$^{th}$ house indicates strong sensual and sexual influences. Many times this can cause scandalous affairs. President Clinton's scandalous affair with Monica Lewinsky occurred when his natal 8$^{th}$ house Moon was transiting by Saturn. Saturn will surface the truth and teaches lessons we must learn as in scandals. This involves acts that go against the laws of nature such as lying, cheating, stealing, or killing.

## Money through others: Inheritance, Wills and Divorce

This is the house of money that comes through others such as inheritances, wills, insurance policies, tax returns, divorce and even lotteries. Money that comes from these life circumstances usually has a price, such as death or divorce. Even the results of a lottery win can have destructive repercussions.

The 2nd house is your personal money and wealth. The opposing 8th house is money you share, or receive through other people. It is the house of your partner's money. It can indicate the financial situation or status of your spouse. Powerful planets here will indicate a wealthy partner.

## 6th and 8th House
### Acute/Chronic Health Problems and Debt/Bankruptcy

Both the 8th and 6th houses concern health and money. The 6th house is the house of health, disease and illness but concerns acute diseases while the 8th house is chronic and long-term sickness. The 8th house is also the house of surgery, which is an extreme measure to repair the body. And while the 6th house is the house of debts the 8th house is the house of bankruptcy. Both houses 6 and 8 are dusthana pertaining to suffering, but the 6th house is upachaya meaning it has the recuperative powers to improve and get better. The 8th house does not get better for it is the house of death.

### Five stages of Death and Dying - the process of the 8th House

At some point we must surrender to the realization that ultimately we must die. There are five stages of emotional transition discussed by Elizabeth Kubler Ross in the *"Five stages of death and dying"*: denial, anger, bargaining, depression and surrender. These are all experiences processed through the 8th house.

### Reproductive and Elimination Organs

The part of the body ruled by the 8th house and Scorpio is the reproductive organs and health problems of the internal reproductive organs. The 7th house and Libra rules the external reproductive system. Furthermore, the 8th house and Scorpio rules elimination such as the colon. Symbolically this refers to the need to release and let go in order to cleanse and grow. To hold on to toxins and waste will pollute and poison our bodies and our lives.

## Bhavat Bhavam
### The Eighth House

It is the 8th from the 1st.

It is the 1st from the 8th. The core meaning of the 8th house is **change and transformation**. All the other meanings steam off of this basis. Death just happens to be the most major transformation we make in a lifetime. This is the house of birth and death. A transformation always means something dies to a new life. This can refer to endings that make way for new beginnings in our life. The deviations that are attributed to the 8th house such as obsessions, addictions, and compulsions come from our inability to change. We become fixated and resist the inevitable changes. Change is not hard; it is our resistance to change that makes it so difficult on ourselves. Issues of control become a part of the mechanisms to advert necessary changes. As we feel a sense of control we feel empowered, but it is an illusion, because we can never be completely in control when nothing here is eternal. Control over other people comes through money, power and sex. These are the vices of the 8th house. Feelings of disgrace and shame come from the abuses of these issues for it is a true sign of weakness to feel the need to control others. The more you try to be in control the more out of control you become. This is exemplified in eating disorders. So, the key to the 8th house is surrender. This is what is necessary to allow change and transformation.

**It is the 9th from the 12th house.** This is the house of spirituality from truth. It is what we learn from loss and learning to forgive. It is foreign travels possibly for spiritual reasons.

**It is the 12th from the 9th house.** It is our disbelief in spirituality or loss of our beliefs.

**It is the 10th from the 11th house.** It is jobs offered from friends or large organizations, it is our ultimate rewards.

**It is the 11th from the 10th house.** It is the friends or associations we acquire from our careers. It is large gains from our career or profession.

**It is the 2nd from the 7th house.** This is the house of our spouse's money or wealth. It can also indicate the wealth of our business partners.

**It is the 7th from the 2nd house.** This is the money we share with our spouse or business partners.

**It is the 3rd from the 6th house.** This is the will power it takes to change. It can indicate commuting to work, also our communications with our employees.

**It is the 6th from the 3rd house.** This can indicate trouble from siblings or competitors. It can also indicate our sibling's health and sickness.

**It is the 4th from the 5th house.** This is the house for happiness from children. It is property and security from children especially the first-born.

**It is the 5th from the 4th house.** This is the advice given from our mother. It can also be money made from securities and real estate.

## Planets placed in 8th house Natal or Transiting

### Sun

Test of humility comes through disgrace. Power and self-confidence may be sought through unethical means. But determination to overcome this tendency will be rewarded with real power. There is shame and resentment associated with the father.

### Moon

Emotions run deep with memories of past conditioning give a profound sense of self. There is difficult early childhood due to mother's perplexing issues. Intuition and psychic ability give insight into different worlds and a different way to view life's experiences.

### Mercury

Mercury is the only planet that prospers in the 8th house! Mercury/Hermes was the only god allowed to venture into the underworld and return. Deep perception uncovers the truth. Life involves research that could lead to scientific discoveries.

### Venus

Intense need for love instigates a continual search for a soul mate in the wrong places. There may be disappointment with betrayal in love relationships. Money comes from marriage or divorce.

### Mars

There is an intense desire to research and unlock worldly secrets. Profound intelligence and the study of spiritual sciences indicate metaphysical studies. There is the use of powers that can destroy or heal. Suppressed anger motivates rash decisions. Extreme problems or separation with siblings may indicate loss or death.

### Jupiter

There is a deep quest to understand the meaning and workings of the Universe. Wealth comes from the marriage partner. Children may cause loss, problems and great expenses.

## Saturn

This indicates a long life. There is a search for meaning through life. Wisdom is cultivated through life experience, a wise old soul. Financial Loss comes from the spouse. Struggle ensues through life to find the life's work and career. Ultimately they become weary with the superficial ways of the world.

## Rahu

There is an obsessive-compulsive need to be in control, which disturbs the life. Sexual powers and are used to attract sick relationships. Addictions control the life. An inflated sense of power can cause abuse. Surrender is the message that can heal the life.

## Ketu

Deep spiritual knowledge, introspection or escape from the material world is the spiritual message of this life. Death experiences, such as a near death experience can transform and change perception. Psychic abilities give connection to other dimensions.

# Ruler of the 8th House in the

## 8th House

Deep psychological awareness can breed constant self-analysis. This is the placement brings intuition and psychic abilities. But a great interest in life after death may predominate life.

## 9th House

Interest in metaphysical sciences gives deep perception and understanding. There is an interest to understand the purpose and meaning of life from a spiritual perspective. Spiritual teachers may disappoint and try to control you. Be careful of cults.

## 10th House

Powers to discover answers to fix and change problems within businesses is an innate gift. Be careful of problems within the work concerning superiors. Research and detective work are a gift.

## 11th House

Friends are not supportive and can create problems due to jealousy. Be careful of not to share intimate information for they may use it later. There is a love of underground groups and organizations that create change in the community.

## 12th House

Gains can come after problems and loss. Spirituality comes from seeking peace after long trials and tribulations. Travel to foreign lands is part of self-discovery. An awakening will come after a dark night of the soul.

## 1st House

Life began from a challenging place, with sickness, turbulent childhood or a difficult birth. Health problems are inherent. There is an unknown secret concerning birth.

## 2nd House

Money problems plague the life. Inherited money causes much grief. A certain issue that concerns money robs family happiness and peace. Divorce and quarrels are because of money problems.

## 3rd House

A sibling has a very difficult life or may even die in childhood. There is a separation or tension to siblings specifically the youngest sibling. Early school or education is very difficult. The struggle in learning interrupted the education causing isolation.

## 4th House

The mother had major problems, was very sick and could die young. The family was strapped with hard ship and many financial problems. At an early age there was a lack of security with no emotional support.

## 5th House

Difficulties with children cause great mental anguish. There is disgrace or hidden secrets concerning children. The mind is penetrating and loves to invent and solve mysteries. There is great depth to the mind indicating profound intelligence.

## 6th House

Accidents or law suites can bring gain and money. The toll this can take on the health may not be worth the challenges. Be cautious around issues of sexual harassment in the work place.

## 7ᵗʰ House

Marriage and relationships are the most difficult issue in life. Partners are disrespectful, untruthful, feeling betrayed. Financial gains may come from the death of a spouse.

*Albert Einstein* was a physics that developed the general theory of relativity. He was a part of the Manhattan Project where he was hired to develop an extremely powerful bomb. Later he denounced using the new discovery of nuclear fission as a weapon. After the bomb was dropped on Hiroshima he has great remorse over the destruction his invention had caused.

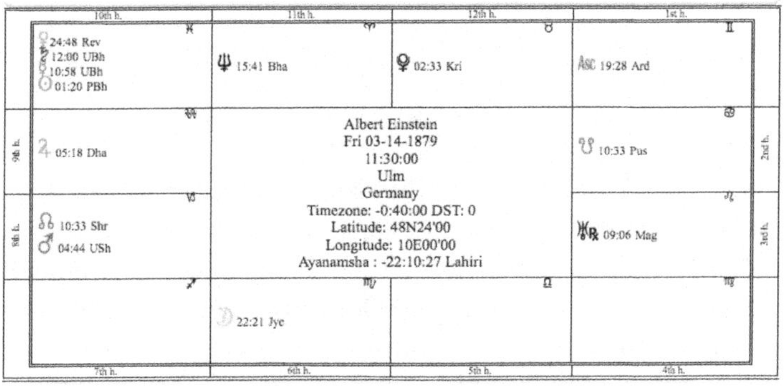

*Chart 21: Albert Einstein*

In Einstein's 8ᵗʰ house he has Mars with Rahu in Capricorn indicating his deep investigative abilities. Mars rules the 6ᵗʰ house of the struggles but humanitarian service and is in Capricorn the most powerful sign Mars can occupy. This is indicative of a scientist. But when Rahu is conjunct a planet it can expand and hugely magnify its power. This is why he has the mental capacity of a genius. As Mars rules the 11ᵗʰ house and the 6ᵗʰ house its will caused problems and Einstein always felt deep regret for his invention because he felt personally responsible for all the suffering the bomb caused the Japanese people.

*Gloria Vanderbilt* is an American entrepreneur and heiress. She was the heiress of the Vanderbilt fortune. Her father Reginald Vanderbilt died from alcoholism when she was an infant. Gloria was called "poor little rich girl" during the 1930s due to a custody battle between her mother Gloria Morgan and her aunt Gertrude Vanderbilt Whitney.

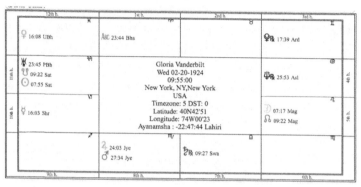

*Chart 22: Gloria Vanderbilt*

After her father's death, her mother was never there to care for her so she attached herself to the hired nanny. When her mother heard her call the nanny "mother", she was immediately fired. Gloria resented her mother. For her nanny was the only one she knew and loved as a child. In adult life Gloria had four marriages and four children. In the first marriage she was too young, and in the second marriage her husband was 40 years older. Her last marriage was the happiest to writer Wyatt Copper, but she was widowed in 1978. She was very artistic and established herself as a one of America's top fashion designers.

Jupiter ruler of the 9th house (luck fortune and father) is in the 8th house of inheritance, with Mars ruler of the 8th house of inheritance. This means she received a huge inheritance from her father. Jupiter ruler of the 9th house of father with Mars ruler of the 8th house in the 8th house emphasizes the death of the father. The fact that he died of alcoholism is a part of the disgrace of the 8th house. Her entire life was about the extremes brought by this fated inheritance. Venus in the 12th house, exalted in Pisces indicates the great losses she endured through life, for Pisces is ruled by Jupiter in the 8th house. She also lost a child and a husband showing the connection of the 8th house of death and the 12th house of loss.

# The 12$^{th}$ House: Escape and Endings

*The self-existent Lord pierced the senses to turn outward. Thus we look to the world outside and see not the Self within us. A sage withdrew his senses from the world of change and, seeking immortality, looked within and beheld the deathless self.*

*Katha Upanishad Ancient Hindu Scripture*

**Vyaya Bhava:** Loss, suffering, final liberation, sleep, death, endings, confinement (such as prison), hospitals, spiritual liberation, release of all attachments, release of resentments, forgiveness, places of retirement and escape, ashrams, films and movies, foreigners and foreign countries, misfortune, secret enemies, expenditures, charities, comforts of the bed, watery places, sea or ocean, outer space, beyond boundaries, feet, left eye.

**Dusthana. Moksha.**

## Escape from the World

The 12$^{th}$ house rules ways we leave or escape the world. There are many ways we temporarily leave our everyday routine. The unconscious ways we create an escape are hospitals and prisons. Sometimes we need a break from life and films, movies, daydreaming, sleep, and vacations give relief. An escape from the past and confines of the environment may take one to foreign countries.

## How we Escape, Conscious and Unconscious

There are conscious and unconscious ways we leave this world. Conscious ways are escape through films, movies, vacations, ashrams, convents, and religious cults that exclude the world. Generally ways that we leave the world based on not facing our problems can only push the problems to a deeper level. The problems will fester into resentments that control our behavior on an unconscious level. The 12th house rules the unconscious, which inhabits the mechanisms in our mind that motivate our behavior. Clues of deep-rooted fears are symbolically revealed through our dreams when we sleep. The 12th house rules dreams and sleep.

## Controlled by the Past

Because the 12th house is the past and pertains to emotions, difficult planets here can lock someone into being controlled by their past. They must work on detachment.

## Vacations are a Needed Escape

Another means of escape that can change our perspective are vacations, which get us away from our routine. We are more objective when we break the monotony and see things from a different vantage point.

## Movies, Film and Neptune

Brief escapes from our world can be in the form of movies, which are a reflection of our world through illusionary images projected in photography ruled by Neptune. Many famous movie stars have a powerful 12th house for they can cast themselves into imaginary roles and become the roles that they are playing.

## Final Frontier, Astronauts and Astronomers

The 12th house is the end of the chart and zodiac (Pisces), therefore it is the edge beyond this world. This is the final frontier as in space for it is beyond this world. Astronauts and astronomers have a strong 12th house for they think outside the limits of this world, which is the 12th house.

As the final frontier, it takes in the vast horizons of space travel and discoveries beyond this world. This is a journey into the other dimensions, space, or higher consciousness. Many astronauts and astronomers have powerful 12th house planets.

## Professors, Study and Research

Professors who spend much of their life in study and research have planets in the 12th house because when the 12th house is strong you feel the need to isolate yourself in a world of research and study. This is a very individual act to explore the realms of deep study. This requires isolation, solitude and inner reflection.

## Drugs, Alcohol and Sleep – Ways to Repress Emotion

Drugs, alcohol and sleep are ways to repress emotions and feelings. Neptune is the great dissolver, which means the very thing that prevents us from knowing our truth will be stripped from our lives in order to see the truth. Neptune and the 12th house rule the unconscious. When the unconscious is made conscious we will heal our lives through our emotional body.

## Altered Consciousness

The 12th house is higher consciousness and our quest for altered consciousness. When we let go of ourselves to unite with another we feel euphoric as in the sexual union. This is a part of the co-creation process ruled by Jupiter and the ability to create. Jupiter rules reproduction and the 2nd chakra, the reproductive area. It is in the process of sexual energy that we release ourselves to a wave of feeling and emotion.

## Past, Nostalgia and Remembering

The 12th house indicates behind the scenes or the areas that are hidden from the world, a place of solitude, behind closed doors. It is our private selves. It is our past and remembering past experiences that relate to us through emotions and feelings, nostalgia, reminiscing, and remembering are represented by the 12th

## End of Each Day or Life

At the end of each day we surrender and retire through sleep. When we fall asleep it is much like a death process we let go of each day, similarly when we die we pass into a resting phase from life before rebirth represented by the 1st house.

This is the house of endings as in retirement from a career or moving to a retirement home.

## Surrender

As in the process of finally falling to sleep, the same can be understood as we surrender to death. In this process we surrender all our fears and our attachments that kept us in the chains we self-created in our lives. Our fears and resentments keep us attached to the conditions we experience in our life. But it is within this house that we come to terms with our life's lessons, surrender and let go which can be thought of as a form of forgiveness.

s

e rules the unknown such as our fears, secrets or apparent
me out of seeming nowhere. These are outer experiences of our
dan.. Thieves, robbers, and hidden enemies are people who secretly
attack. This can be people talking secretly behind your back or blackmail. This
is the house of secret enemies, meaning you don't know where an attack is
coming from.

## Hidden and Secret Places away from the Day

The 12th house rules places of the night meaning bars, strip clubs, backstage
or any places behind the scenes, hidden or secret places of escape from the
daylight and awareness. This house is before the dawn of day and these are the
places people go at late night before the dawn.

The 6th house pertains to health and healing professions such as doctors,
nurses and healers. The twelfth house as the opposing house indicates healing
professions too, but on a public level as in hospitals or large institutions.

## Rules the Feet and Left Eye

The 12th house rules the feet. The feet enable us to stand and give balance in
the world. The feet give us the ability to move – walking and running. But a
very specific ruler ship of the 12th house is the left eye. Whereas the 2nd house
rules eyesight and is specifically the right eye, the 12th house is the left eye. The
left side of our body is controlled by the right side of the brain indicating our
intuitive and creative center. The eyes give us sight; therefore this is the house
of intuitive sight hidden from conscious or the physical. This is the psychic
sense to know what is not seen.

## Charities and Expenditure

Giving is an act of generosity and the 12th house and Pisces rule charities.
Loss and expenditure are related to giving which can be conscious or
unconscious. If we give to a charity, we are giving consciously but loss incurred
by gambling is an unconscious loss. Orphanages are charitable organizations
ruled by the 12th house as it is the 8th house from the 5th house.

## Dark Night of the Soul

It is the place we come to as we come to terms with the part of us that
contains our deepest fears, but this is the last phase that brings us to the light or
rebirth. It is the darkest night before the dawn, so in essence it can be the dark
night of the soul.

## The Unconscious Mind

*"Until you make the unconscious conscious, it will direct your life and you will call it fate."*

*"Whatever is rejected from the self, appears in the world as an event."*

*"Where wisdom reigns, there is no conflict between thinking and feeling."*

*"I am not what happened to me, I am what I choose to become."*

*Carl G. Jung*

Unconsciously our behavior will create experiences that seem beyond our control, but on closer inspection it is our behavior that has caused the events due to our beliefs. This has to do with the many ways we sabotage ourselves believing it is our fate. Swiss psychotherapist Carl G. Jung explains, "When an inner situation is not made conscious, it appears outside as fate," and "you meet your destiny on the road you take to avoid it. Until you make the unconscious conscious it will direct your life and you will call it fate." Writer and spiritualist Ralph Waldo Emerson said, "Fate is nothing but the deeds committed in a prior state of existence." These apparent fated events take us to hospitals, prisons, jail, or institutions.

## Unconscious Escape

*"Your visions will become clear only when you can look into your own heart. Who looks outside, dreams; who looks inside, awakes."*

*Carl G. Jung*

Our unconscious behavior creates results that we believe are randomly happening to us, calling it fate. Never believing we are responsible for the conditions being manifested. Essentially it is the violation of the natural laws that will lead us to time out, or time away from the world to contemplate our actions. In reality, our mind is creating our own prison.

## Forgiveness

In our understanding of the word forgiveness we believe it is to grant a gift to circumstances or people who are unforgivable. The question is; how can this be done with the need for justice? This sense of unfairness magnifies more injustice perpetuating a victim. The victim becomes so magnified that more and more loss ensues. I believe this is why the 12th house is the house of loss. As the victim scenario continues, the victim becomes so overtly righteous they actually are the perpetuator of crimes and so called evil acts. The victim attracts the perpetrator by its weakness from continually dwelling on the past hurts and cannot let go of the injustices.

## Resentments from Injustice

This mindset develops within it deep resentments which control and attract seemingly unprovoked events. Most of the time these resentments are hidden and buried from the observer. But the true act of forgiveness is to actually understand the deep core issues behind resentments. This realization comes from the wisdom of why we feel injustice in our lives.

## The Victim

It all begins when others get something we feel should be ours. As we sulk and stew, bigger events occur impacting and justifying our case as a victim and we never come realize we are unable to receive the good of life because we are focalized on the injustices. Many resort to religions as a means of escape from these feelings since religions condone this victim behavior (we are the sinner, original sin, we cannot help ourselves) and we cannot fathom we are the cause of our own suffering. It is our reactions to the stimulus in the environment that magnifies the experiences and circumstances. *We have to come to a place of understanding that it is our reactions to life's situations that determines our results in life. So, to forgive is actually to understand ourselves.*

## "Age of Pisces" birth of Christianity

The "Age of Pisces" began 2,000 years ago with Jesus Christ. This was the birth of Christianity. The message of Christianity is to understand forgiveness but the message has been misinterpreted by the focus on suffering. Jesus' suffering is the focus instead of his messages. "Know Thyself," which means to understand ourselves thus the workings of the Universe are revealed. The visual focal point in all Christian churches is a morbid body of Jesus nailed to a cross with blood dripping and a crown of thorns. This image of suffering and pain is maximized with guilt as Christians preach that he died for our sins. This begins a lifetime of guilt with a belief that the only way to reach Heaven is through suffering. This encourages the victim attitude. It is not only the story of Jesus that promotes the victim image, a suffering attitude for all religions instills this belief. The deeper message of forgiveness is misinterpreted because of the level of consciousness and focus on the suffering. Jesus as "the savior" puts the power of God outside of ourselves and does not promote a message of responsibility. Believing that if you pray hard enough you will be saved instead of making a conscious change in the attitudes that have caused self-created problems. With this mindset victims will remain victims, always casting the blame outside of them giving their power away to change their lives for the better. The 12th house will teach us to release the need to be a victim.

## Wizard of Oz and God

The Wizard of Oz is an analogy of our search an All Powerful God who can give us what we want, to return home. As Dorothy searched for the all powerful Oz, she believed he was the only one who could save her. Her journey through the land of Oz is symbolic of life as we try to find ourselves though our adventures and experiences. She thought the only one who could save her from the perils of this world was the Wizard of Oz. Her entire search was to get to the wizard so he could get her back home. The wizard of Oz is the search outside ourselves for a god that can save us from the perils of this world. Yet when she finally got to the Wizard she discovered he was an imposter. She found her truth within herself and discovered in a quest to go back home that she already had that which she was searching for. With this realization she then awoke to find it was a dream and she was home. Life is a dream and we will awaken to the truth. This awakening is the 12th house experience.

## Where does the Victim Originate?

Why do people want to be a victim? In their righteousness they need to be right. Moral judgments are based on belief systems taught in childhood. As children we have no ability to discriminate and what is taught becomes truth or law. These are opinions of the personality and earthly human laws. The 12th house is the house of spiritual law, not manmade law.

As children we go through a phase where we look at everything in terms of being fair. You can hear the children saying, "That's not fair." But clearly the situations of unfairness come to those who focus on being a victim. This grows into problems in later life. This is what builds the consciousness of the victim.

Victims never achieve their greatest desires because on some level they feel it isn't fair, and never get anywhere in life. They are always complaining, whining, never coming up with any solutions. Victims don't take responsibility for their actions because they are always blaming others for their failures. When they cast blame on others, the power to look at their part in the situation is given away, and no change is possible. It is always the parents, teachers, siblings, and spouse's fault. But it is when we are able to understand our part in the problems that the miracles happen.

## Victims are Manipulative

Victims can be very controlling in a passive aggressive way. They try to get others to do what they want through guilt. They are master manipulators, and when people don't fall for their ploys they go deeper into their victimization consumed with resentments, and anger based on their feelings of personal injustice.

## Realization of Universal Truth

In the 12th house we come to realize past-embedded resentments are the cause of our life's problems and it is time to release the story of the victim. Our attachment to our injustices must be released for the process of forgiveness to occur. Forgiveness involves understanding the mechanisms behind our behavior. Connection to the Universal mind and not the individual self gives this wisdom. The Universal God is where we connect when we free ourselves from all worldly attachments. These attachments come from our personal beliefs taught at an early age.

## Own Self-Undoing

This is the house of our own self-undoing meaning the results of this house come to us as a result of our actions. We will receive exactly what we think we deserve. *We reap as we sow* - this seems to imply karma or the law of nature, which is cause and effect. Our actions give the same results back. This is the time of give back, for good or bad. But self-undoing can imply self-destructive sabotage. A deep, honest look at our beliefs can help transform our sense of self. Are we consumed with our judgments based on beliefs formed at an early age through religious or cultural conditioning? Conscious awareness will heal the unconscious cause and effect.

## Jupiter rules Sagittarius and Pisces

Pisces is the 12th sign ruled by Jupiter. As Jupiter rules both Sagittarius and Pisces both signs relate to spirituality. The 9th sign and Sagittarius represent teachers, learning, truth and laws. The negative side of Sagittarius pertains to man-made laws and justice, and the Pisces counterpart relates to laws of spirituality or nature.

## Neptune and Pisces

Neptune is the ruler of Pisces with Jupiter. Jupiter, called Guru, is the teacher and truth, while Neptune is an ethereal force of beyond this world. Neptune as the god of the seas and oceans is a force beyond our control and will take us on emotional journeys into the unconscious. Neptune is a powerful force and shakes the world with his trident. We cannot fight against the powerful force of nature. We must learn to understand it and go with the flow. We cannot stop the process of death or sleep; instead we must learn to embrace these transitions. This is our exit to leave and step out into the unknown or unconsciousness.

## Neptune

The planet that is associated to Pisces (the 12th Sign) is Neptune which when discovered brought about photography.

Neptune was discovered around 1846. At this time photography was beginning, symbolic of Neptune's creation of illusions that seem real, as in photos or films. This was the onset of screen movies that would connect the world with collective trends and messages. Neptune is about ecstasy, either the "high" received through spiritual revelations or the "high" received through drugs and alcohol. It is connected with intoxication, art, music, and dancing. It rules the illusions of the world, spirituality, and psychic powers. Neptune is the higher octave of Venus.

To realize the illusions of this world we have to go through the emotional body or feelings to understand reality. Everything is an illusion and the only way out is to connect with the Divine which is accessed through the emotional body. This is why the water houses are part of liberation. We are all asleep as Neptune can indicate the ways we stay asleep, stay in denial, escape reality. The only reality comes with awakening from the sleep of this world, and this is where we retire when we die. As we go to sleep at night, we retire from the world of our lives here but we go into another level of consciousness. Dreams give impressions of our inner and true reality in the same way we rest in peace from our lives when we die in another dimension or consciousness.

**Neptune Keywords:** Illusions, deception, confusion, denial, drugs, alcohol, fantasies, fog, dreams, romance, glamour, spirituality, higher consciousness, devotion, cults, the ocean, liquids, oil and gas, sensitivity, psychic.

**Mythology:** Neptune (Poseidon) was the stormy god of the seas and ocean. The Greek myths connect Neptune's meanings to those of Dionysus, the god of drunken ecstasy. Pisces and the last nakshatra Revati exemplify the urge to unite with the ecstasy of the collective unconscious, as the twelfth sign and twelfth house mark the end of life in the material world. Neptune is associated with Pisces.

## Shedding Worldly Attachments

This house is the evolution of the end of life where the worldly attachments are shed. It represents the aging process where the world has lost its glamour, been there and done that, letting go of the dream or illusion and merging with the collective unconscious. The ocean is a symbol of the collective unconscious. It is through our emotions and feelings that we are all connected on this level. It is the final frontier of letting go and dissolving the resentments and fears of a lifetime. This is the final and ultimate liberation of life.

# Bhavat Bhavam

## The Twelfth House

It is the 12<sup>th</sup> from the 1<sup>st</sup>.

**It is the 1<sup>st</sup> from the 12<sup>th</sup>.** The core essence of this house is **letting go** of this world. It is termed the house of loss, but it is actually the escape from the attachments and resentments of this world. It rules any form of escape from this world. There are many ways we detach or escape from this world; life in an ashram, a prison, hospital, retreat, vacation, movies, imagination, meditation, sleep and ultimately death. The 12<sup>th</sup> house rules all these things. It also rules the vast frontiers beyond this world dealing with the vastness of space. The 12<sup>th</sup> house has no boundaries. It is related to the number 12 signifying completion. When resentments are released, forgiveness frees our soul and love and compassion is realized, this is the essence of God. These are the gifts of the 12<sup>th</sup> house. The 12<sup>th</sup> house is the merging with the oneness, not the separation felt in the earthly world. This can be seen as the sexual experience (bed pleasures) as merging with another as one. The higher side of this house relates to connecting to the collective unconscious. It is our involvement with charitable organizations. It also rules foreign things and countries, which are things and people beyond our boundaries, aliens.

**It is the 11th from the 2nd house.** This indicates large sums of money or our desire for wealth and money.

**It is the 2nd from the 11th house.** It indicates the wealth of our oldest sibling. Money gained from friends. Large sums of money given, as in charities.

**It is the 10th from the 3rd house.** This is a career in the arts or travel. It is the career of our siblings (especially the youngest).

**It is the 3rd from the 10th house.** This represents the arms of the government; therefore it has to do with governmental agencies. It can indicate travel for your career.

**It is the 9th from the 4th house.** This house indicates our maternal grandfather since it is our mother's father. It is our mother's beliefs and spiritual views.

**It is the 4th from the 9th house.** It is our father's mother, therefore our paternal grandmother. It can indicate the fixed assets of our father. It is our father's homeland.

**It is the 8th from the 5th house.** This is the house of the death or disgrace of children (particularly the first born). It could indicate problems with children, or inability to have children, orphanages.

**It is the 5th from the 8th house.** This is the house that reveals the depth of our mind. It is our imagination.

**It is the 7th from the 6th house.** This is the house of partnerships in the work place.

**It is the 6th from the 7th house.** This is the house of the health of our spouse. It may be indicative of our spouse's enemies.

# Planets in the 12th House

## Sun

The Sun in the house of loss indicate loss of self-esteem. There are issues with the father. Power and focus comes from investigating the past or history. Love of mystery and intrigue gives intuitive powers. There is a need for privacy and solitude to restore and recoup the soul.

## Moon

Love of the past and heritage attracts one to nostalgia. Nurturing and caring to many is a part of work or a profession. Being overly sensitive can cause health issues. There is a good memory, caution to being stuck in the past. Issues and loss concern the mother.

## Mercury

Mercury in the 12th house gives intelligence and a profound sense of research, study, and is highly educated. There are many travels and interest in other cultures, even outer space. Understanding comes from a deep psychological level, leading to an interest in counseling and caretaking.

## Venus

Venus is very powerful here, and confers wealth for Venus is the only planet that prospers in the 12th house. But there may be disappointment in love, Sleep and comforts are a necessity. There is a good sense of the self and happiness. Sexuality and passion are a part of marriage.

## Mars

There is a repressed deep-seated anger. Passive aggressive tendencies create more problems than tare avoided. Drive to explore the inner worlds and frontiers bring fascination such as Oceanography or Astronomy, Spiritual awareness to alleviate suffering comes as a healer or doctor. There can be secret enemies lurking, make sure there are means for security.

## Jupiter

Great generosity brims over with a need to help others. Healing professions such as a therapist give purpose and meaning to life. There is loss around children or the inability to have them. Vivid and prophetic dreams give futuristic foresight. Love of animals gives contentment and serenity.

## Saturn

There is the risk of being controlled by the past, Must learn to let go of old hurt feelings. Detachment from past, heritage or family, may give a sense of isolation, there is a fear of being alone. Looking within will heal and move one to the truth. The sleep disturbed or shallow, never feeling fully rested, and forgets or doesn't remember dreams, There are bad past memories that haunt them in the night.

## Rahu

Deep attachments to material world can create a self-imposed prison. Deep-seated fears and secrets control many reactions and responses in life causing addictions. There is a fascination of foreigners and foreign lands, Attainment of spiritual powers such as mental powers and concentration can be used for self-gain. , Secret enemies such as thieves and robbers can attack and invade privacy.

## Ketu

Life is about a spiritual search for purpose and meaning, The spiritual quest is never ending and always feels like an emptiness and a void in the life. There is a desire for deep love that is not of this world. Mystical Journeys to foreign lands give a feeling of freedom and escape. Interest in the unknown keeps a search and learning of the metaphysical sciences, meditation, and life beyond death.

# Ruler of the 12th in the

### 1st House

Is very private and secretive, wanting to be behind the scenes, not comfortable in the public eye. Weakness in physical health comes at an early age.

### 2nd House

Can indicate losses financially throughout life, A difficult childhood, can lead to many insecurities latter. A temperamental personality causes distance from others. They are soft-spoken believing no one hears them or that their words are invalidated. Problems with dentures or the teeth come with age.

### 3rd House

Will cause loss around siblings, There is low vitality, drive and ambition. The willpower is weak with no motivation. There can be loss of hearing or ear infections.

## 4th House

The mother experienced losses and difficult life. The sense of security feels threatened and conditions the entire life with insecurity. Problems come from costly real estate or the inability to purchase a home.

## 5th House

May indicate losses around children or the inability to have them. Unusual and unique creativity comes through a special talent. Interest in supernatural cultivates learning and mastering metaphysical sciences.

## 6th House

There is an interest in the healing professions and health matters, indicating a healer, doctor, nurse or councilor. A high Sensitivity to the environment can indicate allergies

## 7th House

Indicates loss and denial in relationships, There are miscommunications and lack of understanding in love causing depression and unhappiness. It is not a good idea to form business partnerships.

## 8th House

Money comes through settlements such as insurance policies, inheritances, law suites, or divorce.. A deep spiritual awareness, give profound psychic ability. They are in touch with their feelings and emotions

## 9th House

There are losses through the father, or spiritual teachers. The father may not be around or is detached. There is a sense of righteousness, consumed with laws and being right.

## 10th House

Indicates involvement with charities and grants as a career. Helping others or the needy is important. The work may be for the government

## 11th House

Unusual friends that may be outcasts consume your life needing attention. Friends are a drain emotionally or financially, Gains come from other's losses, money comes through their destruction or financial loss or repossession of property

## 12<sup>th</sup> House

Deep introspection and psychic ability is indicated, They feel unconnected to the physical world, Great loss and heartache lead to a spiritual search and journey

*Alice Bailey* was a writer and theosophist in what she termed "Ageless Wisdom". This includes occult teachings of esoteric psychology, healing and astrology. Her esoteric thought covered topics as to how spirituality relates to the solar system and meditation. She was ahead of her time with her vision of a unified society and a global spirit of religion ascertaining the concept of the Age of Aquarius.

| 9th h. | | 10th h. | | 11th h. | | 12th h. | |
|---|---|---|---|---|---|---|---|
| ♃ 23:03 Rev | ♓ | ♄ 04:17 Ash<br>♆ 21:08 Bha | ♈ | ♀ 05:20 Kri<br>☿ 25:39 Mrg | ♉ | ☉ 03:16 Mrg<br>☋ 14:17 Ard<br>☿ 18:52 Ard | ♊ |
| 8th h. | ♒ | Alice Bailey<br>Wed 06-16-1880<br>07:32:00<br>Manchester<br>England | ♑ | | | ♂ 16:31 Pus<br>Asc 17:03 Asl | ♋ 1st h. |
| 7th h. | | Timezone: 0 DST: 0<br>Latitude: 53N30'00<br>Longitude: 02W13'00<br>Ayanamsha : -22:11:32 Lahiri | | ♍ | ♎ | ♅ 13:12 Mag | ♌ 2nd h. |
| ☊ 14:17 PSh | ♐ | | 5th h. | | 4th h. | ☽ 08:14 UPh | ♍ 3rd h. |
| 6th h. | | | | | | | |

*Chart 23: Alice Bailey*

As she was so otherworldly and spiritual she has to have a powerful 12<sup>th</sup> house. In her 12<sup>th</sup> house she has Sun, and Mercury in Gemini. The fact that these planets are in Gemini indicates her need to teach her ideas of spirituality through her writings and published books. She has written a beautiful collection of esoteric spiritual books. Mercury rules the 12<sup>th</sup> house and is in the 12<sup>th</sup> house indicating a focus through the purpose to teach spirituality. Mercury is with Ketu indicating a magnification of her presence in spiritual realms in her life. The Sun adds to the focus of her sprit and involvement spirituality as with Ketu indicates renunciation of the ego, which is a part of true spirituality.

*Ralph Waldo Emerson* was a poet and lecturer who lead the Transcendental Movement of the mid 19th Century. Emerson wrote on a number of subjects using his philosophical ideas of that spoke of individuality, freedom, and the ability of mankind to realize almost anything and the relationship of the soul and the surrounding world. His philosophy was that the Universe is composed of nature and Soul.

| 7th h. | | 8th h. | 9th h. | 10th h. | |
|---|---|---|---|---|---|
| | ♓ | ♈ | ♉ | ♊ | |
| | | ♀ 06:19 Ash | ☉ 12:28 Roh | ☿ 03:54 Mrg | |
| 6th h.  ♀ 17:14 Sat  ☊ 05:58 Dha | ♒ | Ralph Waldo Emerson Wed 05-25-1803 15:15:00 Boston, MA, Massachusetts USA Timezone: 5 DST: 0 Latitude: 42N21'30 Longitude: 71W03'37 Ayanamsha : -21:06:51 Lahiri | | ☽ 13:46 Pus  ♂ 16:34 Pus | 11th h. |
| 5th h. | ♑ | | | ☋ 05:58 Mag  ♄ 22:49 PPh | 12th h. |
| | ♐ | ♏ | ♎ | ♃ 04:50 UPh  ♅℞ 16:24 Has  Asc 28:28 Cht | ♍ |
| | | ♆℞ 00:58 Vis | | | |
| 4th h. | | 3rd h. | 2nd h. | 1st h. | |

*Chart 24: Ralph Waldo Emerson*

With his deep understanding of the Universe and spirituality Emerson has to have a powerful 12th house. He has Saturn and Ketu in Leo in the 12th house. Ketu conjunct a planet has a spiritualizing effect. Saturn as the ruler of the 5th house of the mind in the 12th house with Ketu makes the mind deeply entrenched in spirituality and understanding beyond this world. As Saturn also rules the 6th house this has an effect on his mission to be of service to the world to enlighten their soul to worlds beyond.

# Part V

## Predicting Your Future

## Transiting Planets through the Houses

*"Astrology is astronomy brought down to earth and applied toward the affairs of man."*

*Ralph Waldo Emerson*

Your birth chart is set up with your own ascendant, which sets the beginning of the chart figured from your birth time. Once the signs are set on the houses the planets are placed in the houses. The houses they occupy pertain to the areas of life that will be activated.

The transiting planets are what determine *when* events will occur in your life. The transiting planets are the current movements of the planets in the sky, where they will be in the future in your chart will predict trends for future events.

The North and South Node of the Moon, Rahu and Ketu as they transit marks the houses where the eclipses will be occurring. They remain in a house for a year and a half, 18 months. There will be a solar eclipse that occurs 6 months apart occurring in these opposing houses. So both these opposing houses will be equally affected during this time.

### Transiting Planets prefer certain Signs/Houses

If a planet transits to its sign of exaltation, own sign or moola-trikona it will produce stronger results for the house it is transiting. It will be weaker and more detrimental in the debilitation sign/house.

There are some houses that the transiting planets prefer, or operate differently in. The malefic planets Saturn, Mars, Sun, and Rahu/Ketu, do quite well in the upachaya houses (3, 6, 10, and 11). They can cause disease in the 6th house, but usually the immune system is stronger. As per my experience the transiting planets give favorable results as per the following table.

## Houses the transiting planets prefer:

| Moon | 1, 3, 6, 7, 10, 11 |
|---|---|
| Sun | 4, 7, 10, 11 |
| Mercury | 2, 4, 8, 10, 11 |
| Venus | 1, 2, 3, 4, 8, 9, 11, 12 |
| Mars | 3, 6, 11 |
| Jupiter | 2, 5, 7, 9, 11 |
| Saturn | 3, 6, 11 |
| Rahu | 3, 6, 10, 11 |
| Ketu | 3, 6 |

## Jupiter/Saturn Year's Focus

The most important annual transits to focus on are those of Jupiter and Saturn. These two planets will give the overall status of the year. Look to the house in which Jupiter resides for the year, and then look to the house that Saturn is influencing; the area of life these houses rule will predominate. The houses they aspect will also be activated. The slower the planet moves, the more lasting the imprint or experience it produces.

In next few pages, let us examine the effects of planets transiting through different houses.

# Planets transiting through 1ˢᵗ House

## Sun Transit the 1ˢᵗ House

The Sun is the karaka for the 1ˢᵗ house giving force and life to the physical body. Energy and stamina inspire a new exercise program. A sense of self-confidence comes from feeling strong and vital. It is time to get back into action with a renewed sense of purpose. A new sense of confidence leads to career success. Exercise consideration for others.

## Moon Transits the 1ˢᵗ House

Clarity of mind gives power to instigate a new beginning. A deeper sensitivity play a major part in the choices of the direction life takes with new projects. This new outlook on life initiates a different perception of the world with a renewed mindset on how to achieve desires. Visits from the mother or a nurturing female bring comfort and security.

## Mercury Transits the 1ˢᵗ House

Mercury gets dig bala in the 1ˢᵗ house meaning it operates well and its powers of communication are strong. Verbal expressions and a talkative nature is part of the need to communicate ideas and self-expressions. Life takes on an air of fun and adventure. New information comes that can activate the desire to learn and grow. It is time to take on a new skill, take a class and learn subjects. The younger generation gives inspiration to view life from a fresh approach.

## Venus Transits the 1ˢᵗ House

The personal appearance becomes more important as complements inspire a sense of personal attraction. There is a glow in the face with a powerful attractive force. Style and image are important and it is a good time to go shopping for new clothes. Partners suddenly recognize the new appeal planning more time together. The arts and entertainment are important with visits to concerts, galleries, museums, plays or the movies.

## Mars Transits the 1ˢᵗ House

Courage and energy give drive and ambition to take on projects formally put on the back burner. Aggravating irritating issues inspire a force to accomplish unfinished projects. This driving force can accomplish tasks that previously seemed insurmountable. A feeling of agitation with an impulsive nature must be contained and balanced to avoid accidents during this accident-prone time. Headaches or head injuries are indicted.

## Jupiter Transits the 1st House

Jupiter gets dig bala in the 1st house meaning it is empowered and indicates a time for new beginnings and projects. There is sense of a new awakening with energy and enthusiasm that inspire life with new interests. Self-esteem and self-confidence are booming attracting new opportunities. With a new founded freedom new projects become possible. Limitations disappear with new circumstances and conditions for future progress. Excess and expansion can indicate weight gain.

## Saturn transits the 1st House

Saturn in the 1st house will give new responsibilities. There is no time for personal agendas while taking care of others. Exhaustion and tiredness can take a toll on the body. A serious attitude seems to squeeze the fun out of life. Wisdom comes from hard exhausting work, feeling older and more mature. More work is accomplished with longer hours and more efficiently. It is easy to lose weight with more discipline and structure in the lifestyle.

## Rahu Transits the 1st House

Rahu in the 1st house can affect personal relationships due to Ketu's opposition transiting the 7th house. Relationships will be tested and anything repressed will most certainly surface. If the relationship is not on good terms this will cause a break up, but most solid relationships will go through a testing period that will strengthen the bond through growth together. There may be an old love or someone surface from the past to inspire love and romance.

Life will take on a quality of fate and fortune as events change and take an entirely different direction than previously planned. Life will change dramatically for the Universal forces have a different plan. Embrace the changes for they are directing life in a new positive direction.

Losses for the partner may involve major health problems that need medical attention. Career and loss around areas that give confidence will lower the spouse's self-esteem causing depression. Don't ignore these issues for they can be serious.

## Ketu Transits the 1st House

Expect a new relationship, with transiting Rahu in the 7th house. The partner becomes more demanding and difficult to make peace. Extreme behavior may escalate that can break many marriages during this intense transit.

There may be the need to escape the trails and tribulations that plague life. There is a definite sense of not feeling connected to the world or life's experiences. It may be time for a spiritual quest to understand new feelings of otherworldliness. Isolation and confusion give a sense of disconnection to life and detachment. As a loner others sense this subtle energy and cannot connect.

# Planets transiting through 2nd House

## Sun Transit the 2nd House

Money and financial matters are a focus and create unexpected problems. There may be some unexpected expenses this month with the mood to spend. The partner may create a financial drain. Pay attention to diet and daily habits, certain foods can cause upsets or health issues

## Moon Transits the 2nd House

Financial issues fluctuate causing temporary money problems. It is not the time to make large investments. Spend more time with the family, cooking and gathering the family around food. This will bring a peaceful and happy home. Stay away from emotional eating that can cause excessive weight gain.

## Mercury Transits the 2nd House

Financial planning gives a clear perspective on what can be afforded and where the money should be distributed. This is a good time to discuss expectations in love and money. Spending money on learning, classes, computers or travel is appropriate now. Look for sales, as bargains will bring big savings. Business in sales will prosper.

## Venus Transits the 2nd House

Financial matters are on an upswing, with luck and prosperity. Purchases on aesthetic or luxury items will beatify the home, environment and the self. Be clear in expressing desires to receive the desired result. Speech is sweet and touches others in a nice way. The 2nd house rules the face therefore products that adorn the face, like makeup or lotions are of interest. It is a good time to schedule surgery or work done on the face or teeth.

## Mars Transits the 2nd House

Easy come, easy go is the mantra around money these days. Impulsive spending is a compelling force while financial gains are good, just be careful not to overspend. Shopping directs the mind away from family problems brewing at home. Be aware of the power of speech, insulting, abrupt words can anger others. Take the time to sit down and eat, for eating in a hurry and on the run will cause digestive upsets.

## Jupiter Transits the 2nd House

Jupiter in the 2nd house gives financial gain. There are opportunities to acquire more income and expand your business portfolio. Take risks with your investments for this is time to double your economic income. Your voice becomes important. It is time to speak your truth. Opportunities to speak or give lectures open new doors. Clarity in vision and future direction gives hope and happiness.

## Saturn Transits the 2nd House

Saturn transiting the 2nd house will cause delays and restraints from receiving money that is rightfully due. Saturn can manifest money in the 2nd house but it is allocated, so it limits freedom and creates restriction. This would *not* be a time to overextend or there will be regrets later. This is a time to conserve money and work harder, for great rewards are due. Legacies and inheritances are coming but with restraints and rules. Dental work becomes an expensive necessity.

## Rahu Transits the 2nd House

Rahu transiting through the 2nd house pertain to money and finances. This can be a time of gains and losses relating to how money is acquired. The financial situation may involve inheritances, marriage or divorce. Whatever the predicament financially there will be extremes with gains or losses.

There will be a dramatic shift with an unexpected opportunity. Expect the unexpected with money. It isn't wise to take risks or gambles.

The consumption of food or drink may be excessive, surfacing addictive behaviors. Problems with eyesight or teeth may require immediate attention, and costly dental work.

## Ketu Transits the 2<sup>nd</sup> House

Ketu in the 2<sup>nd</sup> house will cause highs and lows in financial matters, depending on planets and the sign in this house. Benefic planets in own signs or exalted in the 2<sup>nd</sup> house will give powerful financial gains, while powerful malefics can cause great losses.

Family life and happiness may change with loss of family members or divorce.

Loss of appetite will cause weight loss. The teeth may become loose and require dental work. There is a decline in eyesight; it may be time for glasses.

Gains in money may come from an unexpected inheritance or financial settlement.

# Planets transiting through 3<sup>rd</sup> House

## Sun Transit the 3<sup>rd</sup> House

Siblings take charge and become bossy around areas of concern. Let them take the lead and life will be easier. Strength and ambition gives an opportunity to take on new projects without any procrastination. Short travels open the mind to learning valuable information.

## Moon Transits the 3<sup>rd</sup> House

Being flexible and open minded brings in new opportunities that open your mind to new possibilities. Unplanned and spontaneous trips give a new sense of freedom. It is a good time to go grocery shopping, follow a recipe or take a cooking class. Gossip is very entertaining but don't get caught spreading rumors.

## Mercury Transits the 3<sup>rd</sup> House

Writing a list of things to do or accomplish will be of great value for the following month. It is a good time to begin a journal. Learning new information comes easy and new ideas are presented spontaneously. A short trip will be prosperous. Good news will come. Sales and shopping are fun and productive. It is time to buy electronics, phones, televisions, or computers. The gift of gab is used it to spread good words.

## Venus Transits the 3rd House

Creative work using the hands develops a new hobby. Composing a letter to inspire someone puts this energy to good use. Decorating and beautifying the home or surroundings bring cheerfulness. Relationships with siblings improve. Interest in the arts, movies, and concerts is a good escape. A short vacation can give a sense of peace and relaxation. Happy news brings comfort.

## Mars Transits the 3rd House

Ambition and drive promotes a new level of expertise. Competition motives and inspires improvement. Athletics and strenuous exercise gives energy and health. Short travels bring opportunities and money. Sales are up and business is good. Arguments conflict and jealousy comes from siblings. Courage to accomplish important goals is achieved.

## Jupiter Transits the 3rd House

Jupiter in the 3rd house will expand the ability to reach people. Communicative skills and talent bring success and opportunities. Travel for work and pleasure unlock new information to broaden a level of expertise. Creativity is at a peak, and new associations with interesting people open doors. Curiosity creates a fresh outlook. This is a time to expand knowledge, take classes and learn by observing others. Taking short trips will build business. Advertising or promotion will spread information fast. Be open to opportunities with television, Internet or any form of mass communications.

## Saturn Transits in the 3rd House

Saturn in the 3rd house gives discipline to persevere through school, hard lessons or classes. Position according to knowledge encourages, education, to learn new material to advance the career. Traveling is curtailed, for important issues and life responsibilities take president and are grounding. Saturn here gives discipline, perseverance and determination.

Accomplishment toward a goal gives a sense of accomplishment.

## Rahu Transits the 3rd House

Rahu in the 3rd house will promote more travel. Opportunities to jet out to new places will satisfy the curious mind. Acquiring new connections will promote future business. Will power, drive and a competitive force inspire the need to improve life's position.

There is a definite change in the attitude and involvement with new people. New business contracts are signed promoting a new level of opportunity.

Business will come from mass communications such as the Internet, television, or radio. Be open to new ways to transfer information. Problems and upsets with siblings may be a major concern.

### Ketu Transits the 3rd House

A quest for higher knowledge changes the approach to people, which will change the direction of life.

Unusual subjects inspire and open the mind. Willpower and drive is low discouraging participation in physical activities. Depression can take a toll on the mind causing a lack of interest in life.

Travel can direct the focus in a new light of understanding. Lack of aptitude and mental focus may cause disruption in school or education. Thoughts in a spiritual direction give life meaning. There are losses or separation involving a sibling.

## Planets transiting through 4th House

### Sun Transits the 4th House

Home affairs are a major concern. There may be repairs or expenses in the home. Family gatherings or reunions bring warmth and happiness to the home. Time spent at home is appreciated. Security is an issue, look into home surety systems. There is a desire to change residence.

### Moon Transits the 4th House

Family gatherings are around food and conversations of the past. Nostalgic feelings and dreams of old times and sentimental memories bring comfort. The mother and her memory may be a fleeting thought throughout the day. Events and people inspire thoughts of childhood. Seeking a sense of security compels home and rest.

### Mercury Transits the 4th House

There is a need to reconnect to family. The mother has a message and will make contact. Dreams are of past youthful times. Gatherings of people meet in the home for classes or conversation. Work brings reading, writing and studies home. Time spent at home is used for learning and education.

## Venus Transits the 4<sup>th</sup> House

The appearance of the home gives inspiration to decorate, remodel or renovate. A sense of creativity invents new color and design. Gardening is a way to relax and surround the home with beauty and expression. Home is where the heart is adding comfort and at peace. This can be a good time to purchase any luxury items such as a new car.

## Mars Transits the 4<sup>th</sup> House

Disturbances around the home cause upsets and problems. Arguments and disagreements are a part of family life, with no peace at home. The mother finds fault and has issues over decisions. Be careful with lit candles or fire around the house, there can be destruction or breakage. Get the car inspected before it causes major problems.

## Jupiter Transits the 4<sup>th</sup> House

Jupiter in the 4<sup>th</sup> house concerns security. It is a good time to expand assets through real- estate, or change the residence. There is a desire for a new home with more room or land. Renovating the current home or to change the look and feel could be the answer. This is the best time to buy a new car. Insurance for the car or home gives security and protection. Working at home is easy and profitable, along with a business on the side. As the house of happiness spending more time at home gives a sense of well-being and contentment. Family celebrations bring fun and gratification.

## Saturn Transits the 4<sup>th</sup> House

Saturn in the 4<sup>th</sup> house will produce fear concerning security and possessions. There is discontent within the family, with losses around aging parents or aunts and uncles. Many things in the home tend to break and cause problems. Car problems can cause economic drain, keep things serviced and insured. Issues and memories with the past will resurface, be prepared to heal and grow. Saturn teaches the most significant life lessons surfacing the realization of what is important.

## Rahu Transits the 4<sup>th</sup> House

Rahu in the 4<sup>th</sup> house manifests many changes in home life. People will move in and out. It is time to purchase or sell a house with a change of lifestyle. The career can determine where to live during this time. Major changes are occurring with work and career.

Life is transforming dramatically. Be careful not to overextend house payments or new items not needed. There is pressure to change the direction of life, and move both the residence and office. Be patient and don't make dramatic changes during this time because things are in constant flux.

The mother may experience new opportunities that give rise and independence. Car problems indicate it is time to buy a new car.

### Ketu Transits the 4th House

Time is spent away from home life. A career loss can move life in a different direction.

There is more expenditure and cost on the home or car. Cars can cause major trouble, breaking down. Do not purchase a car or a home at this time.

There are security issues concerning home and family. Financial matters can cause problems with self-esteem. An empty feeling in the heart yearns to feel a connection to home and family.

Loss around the mother can bring family closer. Family reunions bring back memories and lost feelings. Changes in residence are not permanent. There is a wandering unsettled feeling in the soul.

# Planets transiting through 5th House

### Sun Transit the 5th House

Inspiration to be more creative comes with flashes of insight. With an expanded consciousness it is good to write down the flood of ideas. Children are an important part of life. Advice is sought for a special area of expertise. Music and the arts are a form of entertainment. Sudden invitations to art galleries, plays or movies are a great escape. Dating or going out is a new pastime. It is time to open the heart and find love.

### Moon Transits the 5tht House

Sudden inspiration to be creative brings an optimistic attitude to daily life. Having parties and entertainment are fun. Children can be more emotional and drain of energy. Women look for emotional support. The mind seems to wander, without focus, daydreaming.

## Mercury Transits the 5<sup>th</sup> House

Ideas have to be captured so it is time to begin writing. Incredible information may produce an article or even a book. The mind is full of ideas and needs to be creative and express. New information and discoveries are the bases of talks or speeches. There is a compelling need to teach, a very specific talent that is beginning to emerge. Talking to children will bring pleasure and happiness for they inspire youthfulness.

## Venus Transits the 5<sup>th</sup> House

Artistic pursuits may surface with inspiration to express creativity. Beautiful things, music, art, or creative writing help fulfill a desire to break out of reality. Plays, music and dancing connect to the soul. Attraction and an openhearted attitude bring love or a relationship. It is time to begin a romance. Children open your heart to see things from an innocent and pure minded perspective. Luck with speculation, the stock market or lotteries is indicated.

## Mars Transits the 5<sup>th</sup> House

A competitive drive and fun spirit wants to be entertained with sporting events. It is time to let loose and enjoy the company of friends. Inspiration may come from siblings as they encourage the use of talents. Children can be a cause of concern with disrespect and belligerent attitudes. Aggressive love can instigate a passionate romance.

## Jupiter Transits the 5<sup>th</sup> House

The 5<sup>th</sup> house is the house of talent and intelligence. New ideas expand life and business. This is the house of entertainment, opening the door to new places and people. Sporting events, theater and movies give an escape from reality. Likeminded people validate new ideas and discoveries. Be alert to cutting edge ideas that can make a fortune. This is the house of speculation and investments to make money; keen insights for gains must be realized. This house can also have a connection to actors, film, or entertainers so be open to these expanding opportunities. Advisory positions are offered, for knowledge and expertise is valuable. Children can bring blessings, there may be a new birth, or your children can achieve awards and great accomplishments.

## Saturn Transits the 5th House

Saturn in the 5th house will bring new responsibilities concerning children. They may need college or a car. A new baby may be unexpected news that gives life meaning and purpose. Contemplation of life experiences comes from a deeper perspective. It is not time to consider risky investments or investing heavily in the stock market. Isolation and time spent alone breeds' loneness.

## Rahu and Transits the 5th House

Rahu in the 5th house causes obsessive and compulsive behavior. This is a time of obsessing over ideas and plans. Past memories surface about regrets in the past.

There may be great achievements and advancements for children. Changes in the home may mean a new birth or beginning of an empty nester. Extraordinary ideas come in flashes of inspiration, but beware, for there is a fine line with genius and insanity.

Intrigue with new ideas can transform life. There is an interest in investments and speculation that can give major win falls.

Love of the arts and entertainment bring happy outings and fun. Sporting events bring a needed relief and connection with old or unusual friends.

## Ketu Transits the 5th House

New influential acquaintances instigate a different direction. Children are a source of trouble and concern. Be aware of their whereabouts and associations. There may be a separation with children, due to divorce or going away to college with major expense from settlements or education.

Amazing insights flash visions of futuristic trends that can be very lucrative. Be Careful around investing due to an overly zealous and optimistic attitude.

Obsessions from the past can control the mind in a negative way. Brilliant projects awaken the creative mind. It is time to explore new areas of interest in the arts and creativity. It is time to write that book.

# Planets transiting through 6<sup>th</sup> House

## Sun Transit the 6<sup>th</sup> House

Health concerns become a priority. There is an interest in becoming stronger and healthier. Exercise and muscle building is easier with increased energy and stamina. Work can be more demanding with much stress. A demanding boss and bossy coworkers make the workplace very difficult. It is time to change bad habits.

## Moon Transits the 6<sup>th</sup> House

The health is weak, pay attention to the quality of foods eaten or there will be stomach upsets. The work environment is changing and many people particularly women are gossiping with uncertainty in the air. Animals and pets are comforting.

## Mercury Transits the 6<sup>th</sup> House

Travel for work changes the typical routine. As a messenger for work there is a need to communicate with others. Younger people have a message. Depending on the sign, Mercury could indicate problems with breathing. Nerves weaken your immune system.

## Venus Transits the 6<sup>th</sup> House

Work is fun and easy with the support of well-intentioned people. There is romance in the place of work. A work project requires creative genius, and a different perspective is required. Healthy foods will improve the health, but sweets must be avoided. A pet can be a source of love and comfort.

## Mars Transits the 6<sup>th</sup> House

Aggression and conflict in the work place causes an uncomfortable feeling around work. Jealousy and gossip cause distrust and insecurities. Unusual stress may cause sickness with fevers and heat. Employees are unreliable. It is time to begin an exercise regime and get healthy. Health problems with pets may be costly. Impulsive behavior may cause accidents, be cautious and aware.

## Jupiter Transits the 6<sup>th</sup> House

This is the house of work, so Jupiter here will produce opportunities for more work. A good work environment brings success. This represents support from people in the workplace, co-workers or employees. This is a great time to apply for a job or hire new employees, acquiring the best team and supporters. Interest in heath and diet promotes good habits that motivate the achievement of goals. Prosperity and financial rewards will encourage more work. This is a good time bring home a new pet.

## Saturn Transits the 6th House

Saturn in the 6th house can give more discipline to peruse goals and ambitions. A strong sense of responsibility inspires over work and a tendency to over compensate, but at times no appreciation from others. Confrontations with superiors or business partners disrupt the work flow. While doing most of the work there is a feeling of being unsupported, tired and exhausted with no end in sight. Employees may quit when needed the most. There is a susceptibility to getting sick.

## Rahu Transits the 6th House

Rahu in the 6th house can cause great stress to the physical body. A possible health scare can motivate a change in habits. This will promote better health in the future. This is an opportunity to change bad habits. Co-workers or employees cannot be depended on or trusted. Employees seem to quit at the most stressful times.

Legal disputes may surface providing strength and ambition to win a case. It is not a good time to hire new employees, for there is a risk of thieves and loss through them.

Be aware of secret enemies lurking around the home, take precaution with alarm and security systems. Co-workers may steal ideas and clients, don't reveal personal information. Gossip behind the scenes may cause problems at work, and worries cause sleepless nights.

## Ketu Transits the 6th House

Ketu in the 6th House can cause loss of stamina and physical endurance. Weakness may cause the immune system to be depleted. There is a lack of luster and interest in life. The health must be watched and physical checkups are required.

The conditions around the work place are depressing with lack or support and the need for help. There are powerful secret enemies waiting to steal private information, be on guard and take precautions for protection.

Loss of sleep, worrying through the night keeps the resistance low. Lies may be spread concerning the character. Surprising unethical legal problems may appear. The loss of a special aunt or uncle may disrupt the family.

# Planets transiting through 7<sup>th</sup> House

### Sun Transit the 7<sup>th</sup> House

The partner is bossy and demanding. Let others feel they are in control to avoid disruption. Stay clear of the controlling forces. Don't let others take control and power, quietly get the job done. The partner needs recognition and will steel the show. The maternal grandmother may try to help, but is overbearing.

### Moon Transits the 7<sup>th</sup> House

A change of heart may be worrisome but don't despair because it is only a fleeting emotion. The partner may be unpredictable and may change their mind, vacillating between many feelings and thoughts. An unforeseen lack of security has an emotional effect on the mind. There are changes and chaos in the office with uncertainty on job security, remember things are not as they may appear.

### Mercury Transits the 7<sup>th</sup> House

Communications and agreements for future plans are made with the partner. Connections with younger people will help to perceive things in a different more open-minded way. Take time to find the humorous side of life. Laughter can be healing. Travel plans for a vacation will give a fresh new perspective on a stalemate. Don't forget to include others in any plans, for they will reciprocate in the offerings. Your maternal grandmother may call or be a part of your thoughts.

### Venus Transits the 7<sup>th</sup> House

Attention and appreciation comes from receiving and giving love and compassion. There are many admirers, be open to their sentiments. Powers of attraction are strong, don't hesitate to give invitations or be ready for invitations for intimate affairs. Attempts to get more attention or advancement from the boss will bring a welcome outcome.

### Mars Transits the 7<sup>th</sup> House

Aggression from the partner may seem like attacks on your character. Let them release steam as they are projecting their anger. Being defensive will only provoke them more. Ignore accusations and know they are frustrated with their affairs. Participating in arguments can be a testimony to guilt. Keep cool and the outcome will be favorable.

## Jupiter Transits the 7th House

Jupiter in the 7th house brings love and marriage. Relationships are blossoming and happy. Agreements and expectations are met. This can represent positive opportunities for the spouse. This transit will intensify or bring a new lasting loving partnership. This partnership brings financial support and emotional fulfillment. Growth in business and career are successful. Love and respect is received and returned.

## Saturn Transits the 7th House

Saturn in the 7th house can cause break ups and endings in relationships. There is a heavy responsibility to keep the relationship together, causing indecision and emotional turmoil. The results of enduring this difficult time can be well worth the efforts. Working on your relationship will create a much deeper bond through enduring this time together. The partner is experiencing personal problems; it is important to be a supporter. A business partner will need more help during this time. Saturn awakens reality, revealing the truth of relationships and information needed to make the right choice.

## Rahu Transits the 7th House

Rahu in the 7th house can attract a new relationship. The partner becomes more demanding, and it difficult to make peace. Extreme behavior can break many marriages during this intense transit.

Rahu can bring fortunate opportunities to the partner but the over blown ego can cause distance and separation. The partner is away on travel or disconnected emotionally giving a sense of separation and isolation in a marriage or relationship.

There may be the need to escape the trials and tribulations that plague life. There is a definite sense of feeling disconnected with life's experiences. It may be time for a spiritual quest to understand new feelings. Isolation and confusion give a sense of detachment. Appearing as a loner, others sense the subtle energy and cannot connect.

## Ketu Transits the 7th House

Relationships will be tested and anything repressed will most certainly surface. If the relationship is not on good terms this will cause a break up, but solid relationships will strengthen the bond through growth together. An old love or someone from the past may appear to inspire love and romance.

Losses for the partner may involve major health problems that need medical attention. Loss around career will lower the spouse's self-esteem causing depression. Don't ignore these issues for they can be serious.

Life will take on a quality of fate and fortune as events change and take an entirely different direction than previously planned. Life will change dramatically for the Universal forces have a different plan in life. Embrace changes for a new life directing a positive and new direction.

# Planets transiting through 8ᵗʰ House

### Sun Transit the 8ᵗʰ House

The life force and resistance is low, beware of illness. A sudden weakness can cause depression. There is a low sense of self-esteem. Take time to rest and don't forget to take vitamins. This is not the time to push an agenda on others. Past Problems that have been ignored need to be addressed. There are consequences from any unpaid dues resulting in humiliation. The partner may be responsible for financial problems due to impulsive overspending.

### Moon Transits the 8ᵗʰ House

Thoughts of past humiliation lower self-confidence. Personal affairs are causing deep worries. Women may be a source of aggravation, gossiping, and hiding information. Trust the intuition to make the correct choices. Financial matters with others are unpredictable and cannot be trusted. The mother's emotional stability is in question.

### Mercury Transits the 8ᵗʰ House

Powers of research are vast and far-reaching. Be a breast of the news and what others are talking about for this can lead to the right direction. Be open to ideas and conversations with others for the information revealed can be enlightening. There is a message that will shed light on a past problem that needs to be resolved. Write a list of things that are being presented, this information will be useful at a later date.

## Venus Transits the 8ᵗʰ House

Disappointment in love and relationships ruins trust in partnerships and the ability to make choices in financial affairs. Their lack of commitment and expectations fall short. It is time to renegotiate these decisions. Suspicion and mistrust comes from fear of betrayal. Passion may run high but reality may prove disappointing. Protection and insurance give a sense of security. Money may come from others in an unexpected way, be open and receptive.

## Mars Transits the 8ᵗʰ House

An undercurrent of anger and hostility distort peace of mind. Unfair covert blame compromise feelings by others accusations. Health is problems may surface, check on any health issues for they may be serious. It is time for a body cleanse. Siblings may be a source of contention, settling a financial agreement. Be aware that money shared with others may drain the account.

## Jupiter Transits the 8ᵗʰ House

Jupiter in the 8ᵗʰ house brings money through others. It is the house of inheritances, insurance policies, and money from marriage either through property or divorce. It pertains to money received, not earned. Money comes through legacies or inheritances. Experiences with death provoke profound realizations of meaning and life. Finances and the bank account will increase. Psychic experiences open new powers and intuition. Financial backing and the power to attract investors will open new possibilities in business.

## Saturn Transits the 8ᵗʰ House

Saturn in the 8ᵗʰ house can withhold and delay money. A divorce settlement or the amount received through inheritance will be disappointing. Money issues teach the most valuable lessons. Restrictions concerning money will prevent business expansion; the wait may change the outcome. Control and power will come from experience and maturity. Saturn will transform ideas and concerns about money.

## Rahu Transits the 8ᵗʰ House

Rahu transiting the 8ᵗʰ house will cause highs and lows in financial matters, depending on planets and the sign. Benefic planets in own signs or exalted in the 8ᵗʰ house will give powerful financial gains. Sadness in family life comes from change with loss of family members or divorce.

Gains in money may come from an unexpected inheritance or financial settlement. This will produce money from unearned sources such as divorce, taxes, or insurance policies.

Addictions or mental imbalances may cause emotional upsets and major problems if go unchecked. Feelings of suicide or depression must be addressed. Treatment and psychological analysis is a part of transformation and healing.

Loss of appetite will cause weight loss. The teeth may become loose and require dental work. There is a decline in eyesight; it may be time for glasses.

### Ketu Transits the 8th House

Ketu transiting through the 2nd house pertains to money and finances. This can be a time of gains and losses and relate to how money is acquired. Inheritances, marriage or divorce may bring unexpected financial gains. Whatever the predicament financially there will be extremes with gains or losses. There will be a dramatic shift with an unexpected opportunity. Expect the unexpected with money. It isn't wise to take risks or gambles. The consumption of food or drink may be excessive surfacing addictive behaviors.

Deep psychological work can promote healing of the emotional body and a release from the controlling past. Psychic development opens the mind to new ideas and studies. Communication with spirits and otherworldly beings comes naturally. Interest can give rise to new metaphysical studies.

Problems with eyesight or with the teeth may require immediate attention, and costly dental work.

# Planets transiting through 9th House

### Sun Transit the 9th House

Optimism brings a renewed sense of peace and contentment. A new perspective on life comes from an invigorating trust in beliefs and the spiritual core. Courses or books that teach human development may be the focus, and inspire a change in beliefs and attitude towards life. A trip or get away can give a needed change of heart. Contact with a father figure or teacher will give guidance, and council. Travel plans to exotic places bring freedom and vision. Judgment of others can have a negative effect on future events.

## Moon Transits the 9<sup>th</sup> House

Spiritual guidance seems unclear and wavering beliefs begin a journey to find the truth. Emotional attachments to beliefs are difficult to change. Past conditioning is breaking down as new beliefs are developed. A transformation is occurring like a butterfly. Female teachers or the mother will set the tone for new realizations. The father may be unpredictable and instill insecurities.

## Mercury Transits the 9<sup>th</sup> House

Traveling or learning new information will open up a new wave of information that changes life. Listen to unsuspecting teachers who appear, they have an important message. It is time to teach and be a part of a progressive group. It is time to listen to the younger generation, for a new lease on life. Spiritual teachings that focus on self-renewal and improvement will make a difference. Open mindedness opens new possibilities and opportunities.

## Venus Transits the 9<sup>th</sup> House

A new way of thinking opens the heart and soul. Don't be afraid to go with the flow of new thoughts and ideas that offer a new founded freedom. Female teachers gracefully offer a new appealing way of life. Alignment with the truth and belief in a new hopeful future cures a difficult past. The usual fears dissolve clearing the air for a life of adventure full of mystery and magic.

## Mars Transits the 9<sup>th</sup> House

The ability to trust the inner knowing is compromised and challenged by the authority of others. It is time to break away from those who may be controlling the mind. Father figures seem to demand attention and respect, but with unclear motivations. The ego and actions don't match their words. This truth is hard to accept. Unexpected and unwanted travel takes you on an unpleasant trip. It is time to trust in the heart and forget manmade laws.

## Jupiter Transits the 9<sup>th</sup> House

Jupiter in the 9<sup>th</sup> house promotes prosperity and luck. A mission to travel to spread important information brings opportunities for spiritual growth. The zeal and optimism is contagious. It is time to get involved in helping others as a philanthropist. Marketing may involve publications or speaking engagements. Spiritual information gives inner confidence that leads to success. A new grandchild may be a welcomes surprise.

## Saturn Transits the 9th House

Saturn in the 9th house indicates a cynical but more realistic view of life. Through difficult experiences spiritual growth has transformed awareness and outlook on life. Realization of limits and boundaries will change life's direction. Answers that give life purpose manifest in everyday occurrences. Cutting back on unnecessary or frivolous things is a necessity. The truth gives freedom.

## Rahu Transits the 9th House

A quest for higher knowledge inspires new studies in philosophy and spirituality. Teachers and high-minded studies change the direction of life. A spiritual quest will take on travels to a mystical destination as in a spiritual pilgrimage.

Don't place beliefs in the hands of a guru type figure for their intentions are not pure. There are opportunities for travel to foreign places and interest in different cultures. Education and learning are a passion with a desire to attain degrees.

Legal problems such as emigration and naturalization issues need to be addressed.

The father is a nagging force and may create unnecessary problems. He may need a health check up.

Thoughts in a spiritual direction give life a sense of meaning. There are losses or separation involving a sibling.

## Ketu Transits the 9th House

The father is on a steady decline and his health should be guarded. Retired from work or preparing for a big change, he may be depressed over a recent loss.

Travel to mystical places inspires the need to explore spiritual growth. Unethical teachers or cult leaders may discourage the spiritual quest, but the understanding that a teacher is unnecessary breeds new vision and enlightenment.

New beliefs change the direction of life and bring a deep awareness and consciousness. Past events bring clarity to the future and an understanding of the Divine laws of the Universe.

It is not the time to pursue legal actions or contend with immigration legalities.

## Planets transiting through 10th House

### Sun Transit the 10th House

This is time to shine in work and career. An advisory position is presented as an authority. Now is the time to schedule interviews and apply for the dream job. Expect awards and a possible promotion. As a rising star, the sky is the limit. Self-confidence is at a peak, attention and recognition compliments a job well done.

### Moon Transits the 10th House

Fluctuations and changes in leadership at work may come as a surprise. The management or company is going through a renovation or change. The changes may not be permanent only fleeting thoughts. Women superiors may be unpredictable and send mixed messages. Don't be attached to the messages or thoughts because everything is subject to change. Tomorrow is another day.

### Mercury Transits the 10th House

Meetings and conferences in work are necessary to open up a new line of communication. Expectations are expressed to clear the air for new business possibilities. While plans are developing take notes because the ideas expressed will become a reality. Be adaptable and open to suggestions, especially new ideas and thoughts from a younger generation. All lines of communication must be open to ensure a successful meeting of minds. Business prospects are good keep an open mind.

### Venus Transits the 10th House

Business ventures will change and come from a fresh positive perspective. Look to options that include expansion and growth. Be open to an invitation for an artistic creative project like art, music or fashion. Eye appealing advertisements with design and color can be the missing link to promote a product or business. Woman will be a driving force in the work place and should be honored with respect.

## Mars Transits the 10th House

Drive and ambition attracts a powerful position, just remember to respect the boss. Do not override the boss's judgment, and risk job security. Careful judgment will line up a promotion. Consideration of others in work is necessary but not at the loss of business. It is a difficult task to balance judgments around authorities. The company is on a rise, run with the success, but be cognizant to share the fortune.

## Jupiter Transits the 10th House

Jupiter in the 10th house gives career success. It will produce promotions, advancement, recognition and congratulations from bosses or superiors. It can also indicate opportunities through the government. This is the house of honors, indicating fame or a high position and positive social standing or reputation. If you own your own business then this will be a very prosperous and expansive time. Karmic rewards are granted at this time.

## Saturn Transits the 10th House

Saturn in the 10th house will promote business from hard work. It is time to restrict and slow down expansion and consolidate. Time to pull back and stream line the business to conserve time and money. Saturn is revered as the planet for the just rewards, so according to efforts rewards for honor and integrity are granted. Bosses that have made work difficult, may be transferred, fired or have to leave on some unknown account. This may represent company take-over or buyouts.

## Rahu Transits the 10th House

Expect major changes in the career. There will be an overhaul at your institution of work. It is a time of transition in the career and a new type of work may be necessary.

Time is spent away from home life. A career loss can move life in a different direction, with the change of home and residence.

There is more expenditure and cost on the home or car. Cars can cause major trouble, breaking down. Do not purchase a car or a home at this time.

There are security issues concerning home and family. Financial matters can cause problems with self-esteem.

Emptiness in the heart yearns to feel a connection to home and family. Loss around the mother can bring family closer. Family reunions bring back memories and lost feelings. Changes in residence are not permanent. There is a wandering unsettled feeling in the soul.

## Ketu Transits the 10<sup>th</sup> House

Unexpected career shifts can give great rise to success, an adaptable attitude is necessary. This career move will have a major effect on your surroundings, requiring a major move. This means many changes in home life. The career can determine where to live during this time

People will move in and out of the home. It is time to purchase or sell a house with a lifestyle change. Be careful not to overextend house payments or new items not needed. Be patient and don't make dramatic changes during this time because they will not last.

The mother may experience new opportunities that give rise and independence. Car problems may indicate it is time to buy a new car.

# Planets transiting through 11<sup>th</sup> House

## Sun Transits the 11<sup>th</sup> House

Powerful people revered as influential authority figures offer help. Friendships with important people and social circles broaden. Respected leaders or the father will give the career a boost. Opportunities for growth are presented in the community. Friends are a focus bringing new opportunities, but they may have ulterior motives looking out for themselves. There may be difficult news concerning the mother or the oldest sibling is demanding.

## Moon Transits the 11<sup>th</sup> House

Friends seem to call needing attention and council. Take a step back from frivolous attention. Don't let friends cause emotional drain, with demands or needs. They will change their minds and disappear. Social events with acquaintances are fun but superficial. Don't pay attention to gossiping women, they are a waste of time.

## Mercury Transits the 11<sup>th</sup> House

Friends call with interesting news, talking excessively on the phone. Connecting to a new group of people with progressive thoughts and ideas is inspiring. Be open to the ideas of young people for they are the wave of the future. Pay attention to a message that brings hope for a better future. Optimism will bring new gains and prosperity. The elder sibling has something important to say, be aware and listen.

## Venus Transits the 11th House

Financial gains are the result of recent career success, reaping rewards from a recent business transaction. Friendships bring a deep connection and love. Accept the gifts they give for they are returning a favor. A friend has a love connection. There are many fun social events and parties that bring new friendships. Attending artistic affairs such as openings for art galleries, fashion shows, plays or movies will add to the richness of life and is entertaining.

## Mars Transits the 11th House

Be careful who may pretend to be a friend, a secret enemy is lurking. Jealousy and contempt may bring bad behavior. Don't confide secrets or there may be regrets. Careful what is said around the office, backstabbing can destroy your career. Older siblings may be defensive, keep a distance from them. The mother may be under stress and needs medical attention.

## Jupiter Transits the 11th House

Jupiter in the 11th house of great gains brings large sums of money possibly from the career. This money comes in large lump sum amounts. This can pertain to real estate deals, selling a business or bonuses. It results from efforts and talent. Wealth and money can manifest out of deals made with associates and friends. Important and powerful people will assist during this time. Influential people come through social events.

## Saturn Transits the 11th House

Saturn in the 11th house clears out unnecessary relationships and friends. The truth and reality about people will surface, weeding out friendships. Friends disappoint and drain energy. There is a sense of isolation and loneness. The 11th house indicates the ultimate desires and Saturn will finalize and build the foundation to manifest goals. Disappointment over past achievements motivates and initiates a transformation to reach peak performance and desires. The realization of meaningful goals and aspirations will manifest now.

## Rahu Transits the 11th House

New influential acquaintances will instigate a different direction. Powerful friends give desired opportunities. Connections are the source of the new founded success.

This is a time of great gains from productivity and advancement in the career. Money in the form of bonuses or promotions comes in large payments.

Children are a source of trouble and concern. Be aware of their whereabouts and associations. There may be a separation with children, due to divorce or going away to college with major expense from settlements or education.

Amazing insights flash with visions of futuristic trends that can be very lucrative. Be Careful around overly zealous and optimistic investing. Obsessions from the past can control the mind in a negative way. Brilliant projects awaken the creative mind. It is time to explore new areas of interest in the arts and creativity. It is time to write that book.

## Ketu Transits the 11th House

Unusual and unconventional friends disturb and hamper better judgment. Don't be persuaded by unscrupulous ideas. If it appears too good to be true than it is too good to be true.

It is time to socialize in the political arena, pay attention to humanitarian causes and charities for the betterment of humanity.

This is a time of obsessing over ideas and plans. There are great achievements and advancements for children. Changes occur on the home front with possible new births or an empty nester.

Extraordinary ideas come in flashes of inspiration but beware there is a fine line with genius and insanity. Intrigue with new ideas can transform the life. There is an interest in investments and speculation that may bring major win falls. Love of the arts and entertainment bring happy outings and fun. Sporting events bring a needed relief and connection with old or unusual friends.

# Planets transiting through 12ᵗʰ House

## Sun Transit the 12ᵗʰ House

Quality time spent alone for solitude rebuilds the spirit and gives time to meditate and find peace. It is time to retire and bring closure to many projects. Children may be a source of emotional drain and sadness. Past memories are awakening a new awareness and reality of the changes that have occurred. Responsibility and worry for others gives sleepless nights.

## Moon Transits the 12ᵗʰ House

Memories of the past and childhood creep into the mind. Daydreaming of sentimental times and loved ones is consuming. Children and their life conditions are a concern. Keep a dream journal, a message will be revealed. It is easier to release past emotional pain that controls life.

## Mercury Transits the 12ᵗʰ House

Thoughts of old friends intuit a sudden call out of the blue. Psychic and mental telepathy is developed with others. Interest in foreign places and cultures may initiate plans for foreign travels. It is time to begin a journal to process and heal a painful past. Understanding, compassion and forgiveness heals life.

## Venus Transits the 12ᵗʰ House

Memories of past relationships bring happiness and sentimental love into life. Content with life, good things begin to manifest. Compassion and love fill the heart and the need to help others comes through generosity of charitable organizations. Love given and received from others is genuine and pure. Travel to a distant foreign place in the comfort and luxury. Peaceful sleep refreshes the body and mind. This is a happy and fulfilling transit.

## Mars Transits the 12ᵗʰ House

Secret enemies are lurking behind the scenes, be careful and don't be vulnerable. Protect the home from thieves with a security system. At work there are those who are jealous, be careful what is shared in confidence to avoid backstabbing. Sleep is disturbed wakening up with nightmares and worries. It is time to take care of the health and avoid stress.

## Jupiter Transits the 12<sup>th</sup> House

Jupiter in the 12<sup>th</sup> house is about endings, closure and finalization. It is time to bring things to an end and may indicate retirement from lifelong work, ending a career. It is not the time to begin a new business, but is time to close one out. Memories and secrets of the past give a gift of self-discovery. Unresolved issues surface for healing, uncovering history. This can be a joyful time of retirement sending off on a well-deserved vacation or mysterious journey abroad. Sometimes it can represent businesses associated with trade and foreign counties. It is a time to prepare for a brand new beginning that is about to occur, as one door closes another will open.

## Saturn Transits the 12<sup>th</sup> House

Saturn in the 12<sup>th</sup> house is usually a time of endings, affecting all areas of life. This is usually not a pleasant experience because hidden issues of the past surface and must be addressed. Final closure like ailing parents may pass or children leave home. It is an end to a cycle of life. Experiences and events of the past can surface shame and regret. Saturn is reality and when it transits the house of self-undoing it can surface old hurts or pain buried long ago. This is a transformational time and necessary for spiritual development. The shadow selves conquer many psychological problems. This clearing is a preparation for a new phase of life.

## Rahu Transits the 12th House

There are powerful secret enemies waiting to steal private information, be on guard and take precautions for protection. Thieves and robbers may be the cause of losses. Stay away from seedy dark places. Loss of sleep worrying through the night keeps the resistance low. Lies may be spread about the character. Surprising unethical legal problems may appear.

Rahu in the 12th House can cause loss of stamina and physical endurance. Weakness may cause the immune system to be depleted. There is a lack of luster and interest in life.

The health must be watched and physical checkups are required. The conditions around the work place are depressing with lack of support and the need for help. The loss of a special aunt or uncle may disrupt the family.

## Ketu Transits the 12th House

Be aware of secret enemies lurking around the home, take precaution with alarm and security systems. Co-workers may steal ideas and clients, don't reveal personal information. Gossip behind the scenes may cause problems at work and worries at night cause sleepless nights.

Ketu in the 12th house can cause great stress to your physical body. A possible health scare can motivate a change in habits. This will promote better health in the future. This is an opportunity to change bad habits. There may be visits to the hospital.

Co-workers or employees cannot be depended on or trusted. Employees seem to quit at the most stressful times. Legal disputes may surface providing the strength and ambition to win a case. It is not a good time to hire new employees for there is a risk of thieves and loss through them.

People may come back from the past to revive old memories.

# Favorite Quotes

*"Astrology is a fact, in most instances. But astrological aspects are but signs, symbols. No influence is of greater value or of greater help than the will of an individual."*

*Edgar Cayce*

*"Occasionally I told astrologers to select my worse periods, according to planetary indications, and I would still accomplish what ever task I set myself. It is true that my success at such times has been preceded by extraordinary difficulties. But my conviction has always been justified: faith in divine protection, and right use of man's God-given will, are forces more formidable than are influences flowing from the heavens."*

*Paramahansa Yoganada*

*"The message boldly blazed across the heavens at the moment of birth is not meant to emphasize fate-the result of past good and evil-but to arouse man's will to escape from his universal thralldom. What he has done, he can undo. None other than himself was the instigator of the causes of whatever effects are now prevalent in his life. He can overcome any limitation, because he possesses spiritual resources that are not subject to planetary pressure."*

*"The deeper the Self-realization of a man, the more he influences the whole universe by his subtle spiritual vibrations, and the less he himself is affected by the phenomenal flux."*

*Yukteswar*

*"Our free will is more powerful than any force outside ourselves"*
*"We are in control of our own destiny by our own choices."*

*"We are not the victims, we are the co-creators of our own world, and can create a better world for all."*

*"We can change the world by changing ourselves."*

*Joni Patry*

# Author

**Other astrological books by Joni Patry:**

Eastern Astrology for Western Minds

How to Make Money Using Astrology

Secrets of Prediction

**Joni Patry Contact Information:**

joni@galacticcenter.org

www.GalacticCenter.org

www.JoniPatry.com

www.GetAstrologicNow.com

www.AstrologicMagazine.com

YouTube Channel: JoniPatry

GetAstrologicNow

Facebook: Joni Patry Vedic Astrologer

Twitter: @jonipatry

Joni is one of the most recognized teachers and Vedic astrologers in America. She was a faculty member for ACVA, CVA and Instructor for online certification programs, published many books, journals and appeared on national and international television shows. As the keynote speaker for international conferences, she has a Japanese website, writes for Saptarishi in India, Faces in Turkey, Galactic Center, and her own online magazine AstroLogic. Her specialties include books and websites for world and financial prediction.

# Notes

# Notes

# Notes

Made in the USA
Monee, IL
22 October 2020